Issues in Education

GENERAL EDITOR: PHILIP HILLS

Outdoor Education

Nicholas P. Gair

Outdoor Education
Theory and Practice

CASSELL

London and Washington

Cassell
Wellington House
125 Strand
London WC2R 0BB

PO Box 605
Herndon
VA 20172

First published 1997

British Library Cataloguing-in-Publication Data
A catalogue record for this book is available from the British Library.

ISBN 0–304–33943–1 (hardback)
0–304–33944–X (paperback)

The extract from 'The Road Not Taken' is from *The Poetry of Robert Frost*, edited
by Edward Connery Latham, Copyright 1944 by Robert Frost, Copyright 1916,
© 1969 by Henry Holt and Company, Inc. Reprinted by permission of Henry Holt
and Company, Inc.

Typeset by Keystroke, Jacaranda Lodge, Wolverhampton
Printed and bound in Great Britain by Redwood Books, Trowbridge, Wiltshire

Contents

Series Editor's Foreword:
The purpose of this series

The educational scene is changing rapidly. This change is being caused by a complexity of factors which include a re-examination of present educational provision against a background of changing social and economic policies, new forms of testing and assessment, the National Curriculum, local management of schools involving greater participation by parents, and the various recent Education Reports.

As the educational process is concerned with every aspect of our lives and our society both now and for the future, it is of vital importance that all teachers, teachers in training, administrators and educational policy-makers should be aware of and informed on current issues in education.

This series of books is thus designed to inform on current issues, look at emerging ones, and to give an authoritative overview which will be of immense help to all those involved in the education process.

Philip Hills
Cambridge

Foreword

Nick Gair has been involved with expedition training within schools and youth groups for over twenty years; he was, from 1983 to 1991, National Operations Officer for The Duke of Edinburgh's Award, during which time he was a member of many national committees relating to Outdoor Education. He also edited the Award publications *Expedition Guide* and *Land Navigation*. Nick holds several National Governing Body awards in outdoor activities and has worked in secondary, further and higher education.

At a time when adventurous activities are under public scrutiny, we should all take the opportunity to review our operational procedures and follow examples of best practice. Only in this way will we provide stimulating programmes of Outdoor Education for young people within a controlled framework of safety.

Outdoor Education: Theory and Practice is a welcome addition to the literature associated with Outdoor Education. It raises many issues over the planning and delivery of outdoor programmes and will be of interest equally to the practitioner and the educational manager, within both the statutory and voluntary sectors. There is much useful advice to be gleaned from Nick's approach to the subject.

Michael F. Hobbs, CBE
Director
The Duke of Edinburgh's Award

Introduction

Travel, in the younger sort
is a part of education;
in the elder,
a part of experience.
He that travelleth into a country
before he hath some entrance
into the language,
goeth to school,
and not to travel.

Francis Bacon, *Of Travel* (1618)

April 1996 saw the introduction of legislation under the Young Persons' Safety Act 1995 to regulate providers of adventurous outdoor activities to young people. This legislation, following the Lyme Bay canoe tragedy, will have repercussions to schools, youth services and other organizations which offer outdoor activities as part of their programmes of personal and social education.

This book aims to put forward an approach to Outdoor Education which focuses on the educational value of learning in the outdoors. It aims to provide teachers and youth workers with a methodology which allows them to use 'soft' skills such as party management, leadership, planning, problem-solving and motivation to enhance the safety of young people engaged in pursuits centred around the 'hard' technical skills associated with activities such as expeditioning, mountainwalking and skiing. The framework of learning and support offered by educationalists will, of course, be very similar no matter what actual outdoor activity is being undertaken, while hard technical skills can often, if necessary, be easily bought in from external qualified instructors. It is the educationalist's responsibility to ensure that the maximum value, in terms of personal and group development, is achieved from the outdoor experience.

This book also aims to convince managers in education, directors of education, headteachers and youth officers, of the tremendous value of utilizing the outdoors as a learning resource as so many spin-offs can be seen in terms of equipping young people with qualities necessary for modern-day life. Concepts such as trust, ownership, personal achievement, teamwork, leadership, determination, strategic planning and motivation are all highly valued by the workplace, yet are not 'taught' on the curriculum. These attributes can, however, be developed through Outdoor Education.

This volume will discuss the concept of Outdoor Education as it relates to educationalists and will offer a practical methodology for the delivery of programmes in a style which promotes the desired learning outcomes, in cross-curricular personal and social developmental terms, in young people. As such, it is hoped that this work will appeal to wide cross-section of schools, youth groups, national voluntary youth organizations and other agencies concerned with the personal and social development of young people through exposure to challenging and adventurous activities, such as: educationalists (school governors, local education authority advisers, headteachers and teachers); the youth service (youth officers, youth club leaders and youth workers); outdoor practitioners (outdoor centre staff and local authority peripatetic staff with outdoor responsibilities); and youth organizations (Scout and Guide leaders, Boys' and Girls' Brigade leaders, The Duke of Edinburgh's Award leaders and Cadet Force leaders).

It is also hoped that the book may be of value to those undertaking any of the numerous leadership awards offered by the national governing bodies of sport such as the Basic Expedition Training Award (BETA), the awards of the Mountainwalking

Leader Training Boards and Ski Leaders' Awards as well as students undertaking education degrees with an outdoor component or HNC/HNDs in leisure and recreation management.

There are many excellent publications available dealing with all the issues raised in the various chapters of this book. Many of these are mentioned within the text and a comprehensive list of such resource material is available from the National Association for Outdoor Education, whose address is given in 'Useful addresses' at the end of the book.

This book could not have been written without the help of a large number of people, too numerous to mention individually. However, I would especially like to thank Wally Keay for not only reading and commenting wisely on the text, but for providing me, over the years, with an apprenticeship into the art of joined-up thinking. I am also most grateful to Michael Hobbs for writing the Foreword. I am indebted to my parents, Michael and Daphne, for checking the text and proofs and, with my wider family, for their support. I owe special thanks to all the many friends that I have made over the years through my involvement in Outdoor Education; I value their inspiration, humour and friendship. Finally, I would like to dedicate this book to Dominic, my brother.

Involvement in adventurous outdoor activities is, for many, a life-enhancing experience. Whether it is the satisfaction of having tried an activity at least once or the introduction to a lifetime's recreation, conquering the physical and mental challenges, on whatever scale, is the important thing. As Henry James (1843–1916) said,

> Live all you can; it's a mistake not to.
> It doesn't so much matter what you do in particular, so long as you have your life.
> If you haven't had that what have you had?

1 A shift in discourse: The changing face of Outdoor Education

Adventurous experiences out-of-doors are perceived to kindle the enthusiasm of the young, to develop their concern for others, for their community and for the environment. Such experiences provide the means of self-discovery, self-expression and enjoyment which are at once both stimulating and fulfilling.

It thus emerges that, for young people and adults alike, Outdoor Adventure is perceived as a vehicle for building values and ideals, for developing creativity and enterprise, for enhancing a sense of citizenship, and for widening physical and spiritual horizons.

Lord Hunt of Llanfair Waterdine, KG, CBE, DSO

Introduction

The concept of using the outdoors as a vehicle for educating is well established; the natural environment, and the adventurous situations we can place young people in, has been seen for many decades as providing an inspiring and challenging setting for education to take place. However, recent legislation such as the Education Reform Act 1988, the National Curriculum, the Young Persons' Safety Act 1995 and the subsequent Adventure Activities Licensing Authority have brought about a change in discourse which has put Outdoor Education, and its providers, under scrutiny.

What is Outdoor Education?

We should, no doubt, begin by clarifying what we mean by Outdoor Education. Education in the outdoors (as opposed to

1

Outdoor Education – with capitals) is a term which would encompass any educational activity in the open air whether in an urban or rural setting and whether in a cultivated or wild environment. This, of course, gives a wide spread of practices. At one end of the spectrum would be outdoor studies (such as geography, geology and archaeology) which profit from direct observation in actual fieldwork and which may require exploration in wild or remote country. These are, by and large, catered for in school by the traditional subjects such as geography, history and the sciences. At the other end of the scale would be adventurous outdoor pursuits (such as hillwalking, mountaineering, sailing, caving, canoeing, skiing and climbing) many of which necessitate movement in wild country or on water. It is interesting, however, to note that 'field studies', often associated with the first group of activities, while being more investigative than adventurous, still share many of the benefits found in other outdoor areas, such as the residential experience and an awareness of the countryside.

This represents a very wide range of educational endeavour and, traditionally, the term 'Outdoor Education' has been applied solely to activities out of doors which involve some degree of physical challenge and risk. This, however, has changed and Outdoor Education is now often regarded as an approach or a methodology by which challenging activities and the natural environment provide an arena for the personal, social and educational development of young people. To quote from the Department for Education and Employment publication, *Safety in Outdoor Education*:

> The focus was often on the skills of particular outdoor pursuits and on developing confidence to manage in hazardous environments. Such activities still have their place but the concept of outdoor education has widened. A range of visits, journeys, expeditions on land and water and airborne activities, either for part of a day or for a longer period, is now used as a means of making many aspects of school and college work more profitable for young people. Such visits, especially those which have a

residential element, play an important part in promoting the personal and social development of young people as well as contributing to their understanding of particular subjects and topics.

Sometimes the focus of activities out-of-doors will be on the process by which young people learn and this will have implications for the role of both the leader and the participants. Experiences may be more self-directed and young people will learn from the process of planning, discovery and reflection rather than from the directed activity prescribed by the leaders . . . Outdoor education, with its emphasis on the skills and challenge of living, travelling and learning out-of-doors, has close affinities with environmental education which seeks to make young people aware of their environment and to develop knowledge and understanding of it . . . Outdoor education provides opportunities for learning through experience and direct investigation of the many features and phenomena to be found out-of-doors. (DfEE, 1995, p. 2)

An agreed definition

The potential definition of what constitutes Outdoor Education is so wide that not even bodies such as the National Association for Outdoor Education (NAOE) publish a generic definition. However, this book is primarily concerned with Outdoor Education in the sense of it being a vehicle for offering young people adventurous and challenging opportunities for them to push forward their own developmental barriers and, in an attempt to refine this aspect of the all-encompassing term of Outdoor Education further, we can see how it has been defined by other educational agencies.

Bradford Council Directorate of Education, in their *Safety Document for Outdoor Activities* states:

At best practice, Outdoor Adventurous Activities are exciting, fun, challenging, inspiring and memorable. Their particular strength, apart from the pure enjoyment of the experience, lies in their potential for encouraging all aspects of the development of the individual – physical, sense of self, with respect to others, social,

3

academic and environmental awareness. The development of all these is probably greatly enhanced by the aesthetic and intrinsic qualities of the Outdoor environment. (BCDE, 1994, p. 6)

The statement goes on to say:

Many school children and youth and community groups are encouraged to take part in watersports, climb mountains or simply make a trip to the local parks as part of a sound programme of education which would stimulate new ideas, develop self-confidence, foster caring attitudes, and provide learning experiences. (*Ibid.*)

Surrey County Council, in their *Outdoor Education Policy*, state:

Outdoor Education; provides a framework for acquiring knowledge, concepts, values and skills through learning, living and moving out of doors; involves a delivery of education which transcends subject boundaries, forging links with a variety of individual disciplines; offers the opportunity to develop awareness, understanding and responsibility for self, group and the environment, thus enhancing the quality of life; is for all regardless of race, creed, gender, disability or social disadvantage. (SCC, 1994, p. 1)

The document goes on to state that the aims of Outdoor Education within Surrey are:

To make outdoor education available to all. To facilitate the acquisition of knowledge, concepts and skills through direct experience of the outdoors. To foster an appreciation of and responsible values towards the outdoors. To introduce and develop physical skills. To provide opportunities for cross-curricular learning. To enhance the personal and social development of young people. To provide challenging opportunities in a wide variety of outdoor experiences under appropriate supervision. To encourage and provide training for people to pass on their knowledge, experience and skills to others. To help people see that activities out of doors can be a source of lifelong enjoyment. (*Ibid.*)

From a youth work perspective, The Duke of Edinburgh's Award, being possibly – through the Expeditions Section – the largest provider of youth outdoor adventure in the UK, states in their *Expedition Guide* that the benefits include opportunities for young people to:

> Demonstrate enterprise; Work as a member of a team; Respond to a challenge; Develop leadership skills; Recognise the needs and strengths of others; Make decisions and accept the consequences; Plan and execute a task; Reflect on personal performance; Enjoy and appreciate the countryside. (Keay, 1996, p. 2)

It can be seen, then, that although there is no one single definition of what we call Outdoor Education, there is widespread agreement as to the educational (both formal and informal) advantages of participation in the activities and programmes we have to offer. So how are these opportunities made available to young people?

The opportunities and the benefits

It is true to say that humanity is on a perpetual quest for adventure and discovery. This is, possibly, most evident during adolescence when the maturing young person is continually pushing forward their personal boundaries of ability and experience and, as we shall see later in Chapter 3, actively seeking out excitement and adventure. Most national voluntary youth organizations and statutory local education authority (LEA) youth clubs are, therefore, aimed at the 14 to 25-year-old age range and it is interesting to note how many of these organizations offer some form of outdoor activity as important parts of their structured and balanced programmes. Examples such as Scouts, Guides, Army Cadet Force, Air Training Corps and the Boys' and Girls' Brigades are well known for their involvement in adventurous outdoor activities, indeed the Scout Movement was founded after an experimental camp on Brownsea Island.

This quest for excitement in teenagers is, of course, not always channelled in such a constructive manner and it is the same 14 to 25-year-old age range which is most involved in criminal acts and which has seen a significant rise in alcohol and drug abuse since the Second World War. These trends are well researched and a 1996 report, *Psychosocial Disorders in Young People*, by the eminent child psychiatrist Sir Michael Rutter and Professor David Smith, found that there had been a tenfold rise in recorded crime in Britain since 1950, committed mostly by young people under the age of 29 years. Such statistics are, undoubtedly, behind recent proposals from central government to invest public funds in encouraging young people to join the cadet organizations of the Armed Services which they suggest will instil a greater sense of self-discipline, loyalty and fitness in Britain's teenagers. The interesting factor, with regard to this book on Outdoor Education, is that the proposals feature highly the positive use of adventurous outdoor activities such as abseiling, flying, rock-climbing and orienteering in keeping adolescents out of trouble by providing excitement and adventure in a controlled framework. The former Defence Secretary, Michael Portillo, who was among the various cabinet ministers (including the Secretary of State for Education and Employment and the Prime Minister) who supported the idea, was quoted on 23 January 1997 as stating that membership of the cadets was a positive thing for young people as it helped them to 'develop self-discipline, self-motivation and qualities of leadership. They make young people team players, give them self-esteem and satisfy their love of adventure' (*The Times*, 23 January 1997). These are qualities which, as we shall see in future chapters on team-building and problem-solving, are encouraged through all forms of participation in Outdoor Education whether through the cadets or any other youth-orientated agency.

We can see then that, for many young people, opportunities for outdoor activity arise through youth organizations such as those mentioned above, or programmes such as The Duke of Edinburgh's Award, as well as experiences offered by schools and local education authority youth clubs. The common element is that adventurous activities are, for the most part, undertaken in the young person's leisure time and on a voluntary initiative.

This leisure time/hobby attitude is, in my view, still reflected in the school situation where Outdoor Education is still seen as largely extracurricular. Before acceptance of outdoor and adventure education as a valid part of the formal curriculum can be gained, therefore, parents, governors and headteachers must be convinced that it is a medium for widening the experience of all young people not just the physically gifted or well motivated. In this respect, the broadening of the child in the whole sense – physical, social, emotional and moral – may best be achieved by exposure to as many of the numerous forms of pursuits that Outdoor Education encompasses as is practical. However, it is not without irony that many headteachers within the state sector, in this era of league tables and 'opting out', are acutely aware of the benefits of established programmes of exciting extracurricula activities in attracting pupils to their school and lifting the ethos of the establishment. Likewise, many independent schools are keen to promote their long tradition of active involvement in outdoor and adventurous activities. And this is not just window-dressing to provide an interesting and attractive prospectus for the school, whether state sector or independent. Recent research by Professor Michael Barber, Dean of New Initiatives at the Institute of Education, London University, has found that extracurricular activities are as likely to boost a school's examination performance as other factors such as the amount of homework which pupils are set. Professor Barber was quoted in *The Times* (15 January 1997) as saying:

> Schools that are setting more homework are also the ones where there are higher levels of participation in extra-curricular education. In both cases, pupils are spending more time productively occupied and less time watching Neighbours or hanging around street corners. (O'Leary, 1997)

It can be seen then that the educational benefits of the planned and intelligent use of Outdoor Education, through whatever medium, can be very significant in instilling in young people attributes considered important by a civilized society. In addition to such social benefits, there are, of course, many significant education advantages, even if it is only the fact that learning by direct observation and problem-based teamwork in the outdoors is better understood and more likely to be remembered than is knowledge transmitted by the written or spoken word. There is also constant evidence that the benefits of self-confidence and co-operation are gained through common experiences in the outdoors. Often these experiences take place in demanding climate and terrain, many involving potential stress and physical hazard. This can, of course, only be acceptable after careful and thorough training and, in these circumstances, pupils are able to realize the importance of realistic assessment of their own resources and the contribution that may be made by other members of the party. Through such situations in the outdoors the need for self-discipline and interdependence upon each other is highlighted and, while it may be success in terms of achievement, physical performance or overcoming a challenge to which the young people relate, the benefits of personal and social growth and competence, as well as increased physical and mental confidence, should be seen by teachers and youth workers as the more important educational gains. As we shall see in later chapters, team-building – including the development of an awareness of the potential and contribution of others – leadership and problem-solving, are seen by many as especially valuable outcomes.

It is generally agreed, therefore, that providing the opportunity for young people to participate in Outdoor Education, and possibly to taste the flavour of the many adventurous activities available to them rather than attempting only to impart the detailed technical methodology, is an important criteria not only so that pupils enjoy the challenge of new and exciting opportunities at similar levels, but also because young people may find an activity which captures their imagination and interest and to which they may become dedicated for life. This imposes two limitations on the potential Outdoor Education syllabus or programme. First it has to be decided what elements, apart from the outdoors, enable all these activities to be labelled together under the term Outdoor Education and, secondly, how the skills needed for these activities can be developed, during the school timetable or youth club session, especially if this is being undertaken in an urban environment where frequent visits to the moors and mountains may be impractical.

The benefits of all forms of Outdoor Education will be clearly seen by those who already participate, instruct or have experience of such activities and who will not generally need to be further convinced of the educational advantages. We must, however, convince parents and other staff how much such a programme could strengthen existing courses and relate to other subjects on the school curriculum. Could this provide an excellent topic for a school or youth service in-service training day? Apart from the very obvious relationships of map-reading and geology to geography, fitness to PE, nutrition and food to domestic science, equipment design and function to graphics and design, flora and fauna of areas to be visited and environmental considerations to biology, many other interrelationships and parallels can be drawn, especially when given the wide-ranging nature of Outdoor Education. Important gains can be made even at fundamental levels. The practical use and applications of maps is a core skill of much work in the outdoors and it could be argued that, through using maps in a practical setting, young people gain a depth of understanding which would be hard to achieve in theoretical lessons in the classroom. Although this is a simplistic example, it is important. A survey of 900 pupils aged 8 to 16, conducted by National Opinion Polls for Microsoft Electronic Publishers (1997), found that, although it is a requirement of the National Curriculum that children should be able to identify principal cities, regions and rivers on a map of the UK by age 11, less than half the children surveyed could place London on a map and more than a third did not know where Scotland was situated.

However, benefits within the curriculum could, arguably, be of secondary importance to the long-term advantages of growth in appreciation of, and a care for, the natural environment, increased personal physical and mental awareness, and pure recreational enjoyment that an 'educating for life' or whole person approach of an Outdoor Education programme could promote. In this respect, it is generally agreed that Outdoor Education offers growth of personal confidence stemming from the mastery of essential skills and techniques which are tested in the safe conduct of exercises which would, in other circumstances, prove impossible. All of these facets are, in today's society, valuable assets for any young person to acquire. As the National Association for Outdoor Education in *The Curriculum* states, these are not unimportant qualities, and perhaps they could, arguably, be

> essential to the survival of complex democratic societies. Sensitivity to the quality of life and concern for conservation are more likely to be promoted by well conducted activities in selected natural environments than by any other means. Yet these considerations do not achieve prominence in formal declarations about the purposes of education. Is this because, so far, recognition of the entirely special contribution that Outdoor Education makes is apparent to very few? (NAOE, 1981)

An educational perspective

Is Outdoor Education seen as worthwhile within the changing face of education?

In *Ethics and Education*, R. S. Peters (1966) asserts that the word 'education' has normative implications and has the criterion built into it that something worthwhile should be achieved: 'It implies that something worthwhile is being, or has been, intentionally transmitted in a morally acceptable manner' (p. 25). In the same paragraph, Peters acknowledges that there can, however, be debate as to what is thought 'worthwhile'.

> It is a further question what the particular standards are in virtue of which activities are thought to be of value and what grounds there might be for claiming that these are the correct ones. All that is implied [by the word 'education'] is a commitment to what is thought valuable. (*Ibid.*)

Really useful knowledge

The current debate surrounding recent educational legislation and the implementation of the National Curriculum has brought very clearly into focus the contentious issue of what is of value, or worthwhile, in education. Much of the thrust of the current debate advocates a return the traditional values of 'essential knowledge' (Holt, 1969). This is the notion that there are certain core areas of the curriculum which are a priority and which should be learnt by all pupils, these core areas being most commonly associated with literacy and numeracy. Holt suggested that:

> Behind much of what we do in school lie some ideas, that could be expressed as follows: (1) Of the vast body of human knowledge, there are certain bits and pieces that can be called essential, that everyone should know; (2) the extent to which a person can be considered educated, qualified to live intelligently in today's world and be a useful member of society, depends on the amount of this essential knowledge that he carries about with him; (3) it is the duty of schools, therefore, to get as much of this essential knowledge as possible into the minds of children. (Holt, 1969, p. 288)

Educational debate since the late 1980s has been much concerned with the content of the curriculum, the introduction of a National Curriculum and testing at certain key stages. Indeed, Stephen Ball (1990) states: 'At the centre of the New

11

Right assertions is a dispute about the valid and true contents of, or criteria for, the school curriculum'. However, Outdoor Education has been seen, by its advocates, as something deeper than knowledge or information. It is seen as an approach or an attitude which transcends traditional divisions. As a Standing Committee of representatives from various outdoor educational associations stated in *Outdoor Education and the National Curriculum* (1990, p. 2):

> Outdoor Education needs to be an integral part of the whole curriculum. It can make a significant contribution to the National Curriculum and crosses subject boundaries. Through first hand experiences it encourages greater understanding of the relationships between ourselves, others and the environment in which we live and provides opportunities for pupils to develop new interests, skills and personal qualities. Experienced-based learning inter-relates with theoretical and cognitive learning. Application and practice give meaning to facts and theory, skills and knowledge are used in the context of human relationships.

The question 'what is education?' has never had two more different opposing doctrines.

How is education conceptualized now?

In an inaugural lecture, 'Education, Inequality and School Reform: Values in Crisis!', Ball, in his opening remarks, stated that:

> The British education system is in the middle of a long, dramatic and radical period of transformation. Patterns of access, forms of control and the nature of the curriculum are all subject to change . . . the greater part of this innovation, pressure and stress stems from the implementation of the many and various provisions of the 1988 Education Reform Act.

The Education Reform Act of 1988 was the culmination of a decade of political influence on education during the long period of Conservative government since 1979. During this period education had been totally reconceptualized and I will, therefore, concentrate on several themes which illustrate the effects of this reconceptualization on Outdoor Education.

One such theme refers back to the question of what is considered 'of value' or 'worthwhile', especially in terms of what is valuable for the education of the individual as a whole person, or the 'educating for life' stance of Outdoor Education. As discussed above, at the centre of Conservative central government assertions was a dispute about the valid contents of the school curriculum which has meant that there has, arguably, been a considerable shift away from the relevance of the school curriculum to the real-lived experiences of the pupil. A return to 'traditional' values may, therefore, be seen as no bad thing in terms of Outdoor Education. Over 50 years ago, the 1944 Education Act had, in fact, proposed that, 'a period of residence in a school camp or other boarding school in the country would contribute substantially to the health and width of outlook of any child from a town school', especially if 'the study of the countryside and the pursuit of other outdoor activities formed the bulk of the educational provision and were handled by specially qualified staff'.

But all is not lost. The final Education Reform Act (1988) entitled every child to a 'broad and balanced' curriculum. One of the underlying aims of such a curriculum must be to prepare pupils for the opportunities of adult life. Achieving this aim depends largely on the way the curriculum is delivered. For example, *Outdoor Education and the National Curriculum* (1990, p. 2) states that

> the trust based on shared experience, perhaps in a challenging or hostile environment encourages the exploration of personal beliefs, attitudes and values. Equally, working in small groups that are engaged in a collective enterprise, whether a science-based outdoor study or a challenging mountain journey, encourages the use of all the faculties of each individual towards the development of groups as a whole.

Much will, therefore, depend on the methods of delivery and the professionalism and integrity of educationalists. As Patrick

Keighley writes, Outdoor Education – as a subject in its own right – may have little place within the framework of the National Curriculum, but:

> Its function and purpose within both the primary and secondary curriculum should be viewed as a vehicle to enrich and enhance learning and cognitive development; as a process by which values are recognised, concepts are clarified; where knowledge, skills and attitudes are developed in order to enable young people to understand and appreciate the inter-relatedness between man, his culture in both the urban, rural and wilderness environments. In order to ensure experiences are not merely 'ad-hoc', these must be planned to be fully integrated within those subject ares where first hand study, out of doors, may be used to enrich theory. (Keighley, 1988)

The changing perception of Outdoor Education

Into the public arena

The tragic death of four sixth-form schoolchildren, from Southway School, Plymouth, undertaking a supervised canoeing journey in Lyme Bay in March 1993, raised the profile of Outdoor Education in the press and media, and increased public concern about safety standards surrounding young people participating in adventurous pursuits at outdoor activity centres and through programmes offered by schools, youth clubs and youth organizations. Public awareness of Outdoor Education involving young people was at an all-time high.

The Lyme Bay tragedy attracted extensive media coverage which continued, after the initial reporting of the events themselves, during the subsequent legal proceedings. The trial found the managing director of the St Albans Centre, the activity centre where the school trip was taking place and which organized the ill-fated canoeing journey, guilty of manslaughter and he was jailed for three years. The case also made legal history when the parent company of the centre, OLL Ltd, became the first company in Britain ever to be found guilty of manslaughter and was fined £60,000.

The catalogue of errors surrounding the events which led to the four deaths in the Lyme Bay tragedy and, no doubt, the subsequent public interest and press coverage of the incident itself and the prosecution of the staff of the St Albans Centre, as the outdoor activity provider, led to a Private Member's Bill in Parliament from David Jamieson, then MP for Plymouth Devonport, which proposed that there should be compulsory licensing and inspection of outdoor centres. This Private Member's Bill received Royal Assent in June 1995, as the Activity Centres (Young Persons' Safety) Act 1995, and the Health and Safety Commission (HSC) were given responsibility for the Act's implementation. This, in turn, led to the production of a detailed consultative document from the HSC entitled *Proposals for Regulations and Guidance to Implement the Safety Provisions of the Activity Centres (Young Persons' Safety) Act 1995*.

The HSC sought responses to the consultative document from across the broad spectrum of those involved in outdoor activities with young people and invited applications from bodies wishing to act as the licensing and inspection authority for the scheme. The Adventure Activities Licensing Authority (AALA) who were awarded the contract, and the final publication of the Health and Safety Executive (HSE) guidelines *Guidance to the Licensing Authority on the Adventure Activities Licensing Regulations 1996* (hereafter *Guidance on Regulations*), came into being in 1996. All providers offering adventurous activities, on a fee-paying basis, to young people under 18 years of age were now legally required to be inspected and hold a licence and it was intended that all such providers, within the scope of the regulations, would be licensed by the summer of 1997. After that it would be a criminal offence for an organization within the scope of the regulations to operate without a licence.

With the advent of the Adventure Activities Licensing Authority, the provision of Outdoor Education was now firmly in the public arena. Once formal, legislative, examples of good practice exist, providers within scope have a legal duty to meet the standards they impose, and it would, naturally, be prudent for those not falling within scope of the regulations, to attempt to meet the same criteria. But where should the scope of such regulations stop? The AALA covers 'adventurous' activities but, if we cast our minds back to the very open definition of what constitutes Outdoor Education, given earlier in the chapter, it can be seen, from studying the AALA terms of reference and the HSE guidelines, that a great deal of the activities which are covered by the description do not come within scope of the licensing requirements. It may be that the debate now focuses on what constitutes 'adventurous' although the 1996 *Guidance on Regulations* sets criteria for what falls within its scope under 'Definition of activities'. While these may be meaningful for outdoor practitioners, many workers without such specialist knowledge may feel the need to seek clarification from the AALA or its inspectors. For example, rock-climbing is an activity which requires providers to be licensed, whereas 'climbing walls, abseiling towers and similar manmade structures designed for practising climbing techniques are excluded from licensing but this does not extend to other outdoor manmade structures such as railway viaducts'. Issues such as this may prove, in the short term at least, confusing to headteachers or governors attempting to act responsibly, and within the law, in seeking to ensure that they use licensed providers for any adventurous activity offered by their institution.

Whatever clarification or fine-tuning that may come about through interpretation and implementation of the regulations, the fact of the matter is that such legislation, and the changing face of public opinion, has brought any shortfall in our systems out into the open and, although there may not be a legal duty, there is certainly a moral duty of care to ensure that all outdoor educational activities are managed to a high level of professionalism. Indeed, the *Proposals for Regulations and Guidance to Implement the Safety Provisions of the Activity Centres (Young Persons' Safety) Act 1995* even went as far as to suggest the formation of a non-compulsory scheme of national approval of outdoor programmes offered by national voluntary youth organizations by the AALA as they recognized that, 'Voluntary associations also want to be able to demonstrate that they are applying the same standards in respect of the safety of their members as would be required for activities offered on a commercial basis'. The advent of the recent outdoor-related legislation is, therefore, the stimulus or catalyst for all those working with young people in the outdoors to review safety procedures and guidelines to ensure that they meet the standards to which we should be aspiring, morally if not legally. If this does not happen, and we experience an incident, the press, quite rightly, will have a field day.

A *duty of care*

Many national papers carried a story on 26 September 1995 which revealed that three teachers from Doucecroft School, an independent special school in Kelvedon, Essex, run by the Essex Autistic Trust, had been dismissed following an incident in June 1995, where an 11-year-old autistic girl had been missing overnight after she had mistakenly been left behind following a trip to High Woods Country Park in Colchester, 12 miles away from the school. The pupil had not been missed until the next day and, even then, the police were not alerted. The official enquiry into the incident, undertaken by David Gane, Head of Essex Social Services Inspection Unit, at the request of the Department for Education and Employment, stated that, although the specialist school was generally well run and had a good reputation, the staff concerned had demonstrated 'breathtaking incompetence' and that there had been 'very significant failures' by a number of staff at various stages as the incident unfolded (Gane, 1995). It may, indeed, seem incomprehensible, to those of us who spend time leading groups in the outdoors, that a party of nine pupils with four members of staff had not noticed that the child was missing until the next day, especially as Doucecroft is (from Mondays to Fridays) a residential school. However, it is not the details of the specific event which should be of concern to us, but the potential ramifications surrounding this and other similar incidents.

This concern should be focused inwardly on ourselves, as outdoor educationalists, in ensuring that we seek out recommendations arising from any incident and incorporate them (if we do not already do so) into our procedures and practices, and focused outwardly on how the scope of any future legislation may be enlarged to cover all activities in the outdoors whether or not they included any activity which is currently defined as 'adventurous'. It is doubtful that the teachers involved in the Doucecroft School incident, outlined above, perceived themselves as being involved in Outdoor Education, as they were taking a class trip to visit a country park, not spending the day at an adventurous activities centre inspected and licensed (as it would be now, but not at the time of the Doucecroft trip) by the AALA. But that is missing the point. No matter what the ultimate destination, any trip away from school or youth club deserves the same care and attention to detail in planning even if this is only at the basic level of developing a procedure for coping with lost children and a system for monitoring their whereabouts at all times while on the trip. Imagine the public outcry, hot on the heels of the Lyme Bay tragedy, if the Doucecroft party had been visiting an adventure centre; it is possible that the teachers involved may then be facing criminal, rather than disciplinary, proceedings. It is certainly the case that parents are turning increasingly to litigation in cases where injury or misadventure has befallen victims of incidents in sporting or recreational events.

One such example is the case reported in *The Times* on 18 December 1996, where a referee was blamed for the broken neck suffered by a 17-year-old player in a youth rugby match (Lee, 1996). The Court of Appeal rejected, as unsustainable, the referee's argument that the player had consented to the risk of injury by voluntarily playing a highly physical game. As we have seen earlier, voluntary participation, whether through an extracurricular activity at school or through membership of a youth organization, is very much a feature of much Outdoor Education and, although we shall explore the concept of risk and danger in a following chapter, this example serves to highlight the changing public attitude towards legal redress for the consequences of any apparent or alleged negligence on the part of leaders or officials.

The value of qualifications

Shortly before the Doucecroft School incident, described above, the press carried stories of a climbing instructor who had lied about his qualifications in order to teach trainee mountaineering leaders. The instructor, who had claimed that he held a qualification approved by the Mountainwalking Leader Training Board, was jailed by magistrates for three months. As the press pointed out, this case came 'six months after the death of four schoolchildren in the Lyme Bay canoe tragedy had focused attention on unqualified instructors in the [outdoor] industry' (Knight, 1995). While in no way condoning this deception, which focused on the falsification of information rather than the legal necessity requiring appropriate certification, it does, however, seem rather ironic that elsewhere in the educational system the use of unqualified teachers is not unusual. The report of Written Answers in the House of Commons for 21 July 1993 makes interesting reading. Mr Steinberg MP asked the Secretary of State for Education 'how many teachers are teaching subjects they have no qualifications to teach?' (Hansard, 1993). The written reply, from Mr Robin Squire, showed, with the use of a table, the percentage of full-time secondary teachers in England who gave some tuition in a subject in which they, themselves, held no post-A level qualification. Religious Education topped the list with 54 per cent of teachers without a qualification, which meant that tuition by unqualified staff represented 25 per cent of all the tuition taking place in the subject. In addition,

19

50 per cent of all craft, design and technology (CDT) teachers were reported as unqualified and the tuition given by these unqualified teachers was 34 per cent of all tuition in the subject.

Although these figures may, of course, have improved considerably since July 1993, it does seem curious that half of all the CDT teachers in secondary schools were, at that time, unqualified and that over a third of all the teaching in a subject which involves hazardous equipment, tools, machines and materials was, therefore, being undertaken by unqualified staff. It is not intended, in this book, to make a political statement about the qualifications of teachers, but merely to highlight, in an era of the Education (Teachers) Regulations 1993 which set out procedures relating to instructors, licensed teachers and qualified teacher status, another feature of the overall educational backdrop against which Outdoor Education is featured. Unqualified teachers of craft, design and technology, while lacking formal qualifications, are assessed by their employers as having appropriate knowledge and practical experience in their craft to impart technical skills to their pupils and there is not the same emphasis on a matrix of desired qualifications for those entering teaching, as there now is, under the adventurous activities licensing scheme, for those engaged in outdoor activities. The term Outdoor Education comprises two words, and it would seem fair that equal legislative respect is given to both.

The HSE *Guidance on Regulations* (1996) recognizes the value of both experience and qualifications in a sensible and even-handed way. The advice it gives would be a prudent policy to follow for any organization concerned with young people in the outdoors, whether or not they fell under the scope of the Adventure Activities Licensing Regulations. Paragraph 18 of the *Guidance* states:

> Providers should provide evidence to the licensing authority that they maintain a policy for the recruitment, training, assessment and management of staff which ensures that all staff with direct involvement in adventure activities (instructors) are assigned to duties within their proven competence. Providers should ensure

that instructors have the training, experience, personal qualities and communication skills appropriate for ensuring the safety of the participants according to their age and taking account of any special educational needs. Providers may demonstrate the competence of their instructors by externally awarded qualification, in-house training, experience or any combination of these. There may be other ways. The licensing authority should accept whichever means a provider chooses, so long as it is satisfied that instructor competence has been demonstrated.

However, governing body awards are a convenient, and nationally recognized, means of assessing competence and many authorities and organizations put considerable emphasis on the necessity for persons acting in positions of responsibility with regard to participation in outdoor activities by the young to hold qualifications and awards of the relevant national governing body for the activity being pursued, and justifiably so. Such awards, as they are progressive in nature, are the means by which a hierarchy of knowledge, professionalism and standards are maintained and are a way of gauging competence and experience. However, educational managers in schools or the youth service should recognize that such governing body awards only relate to the individual's competence and experience at the time of assessment and represent only the minimum necessary standard of technical ability to undertake instructional or leadership tasks. As the UK Mountain Training Board (UKMTB) states in *National Guidelines; Advice on Safety, Good Practice and the Use of Mountain Training Awards*:

> The responsibility for deployment and management of [governing body] award holders and the judgement of the suitability of such individuals for other aspects of their employment lie with the employer or provider [of the outdoor activity]. Such deployment should take account of the recent experience and health of the holder and include further training as necessary. (UKMTB, 1995, p. 7)

Although virtually impossible to substantiate, it is often said that young people working in the outdoors are safer under the leadership of an experienced, mature instructor with no formal qualifications than they would be in the care of a young, qualified instructor, and many governing body awards have in-built systems (such as age barriers or the requirement for considerable prior experience) to prevent leaders holding such qualifications being very close in age to adolescent participants. Nevertheless, it is an issue to which managers in both the statutory and voluntary sectors should give due attention in the selection and approval of staff.

The future

The current climate of educational and legal reform affecting Outdoor Education may have mixed results in the short term. On the one hand, the adventure activities licensing scheme ensures that parents, schools and local authority youth services, have the reassurance of a national system of inspections and approval of centres and organizations providing adventurous activities, on a 'for payment' basis to young people under the age of 18. On the other hand, there is still some confusion over the position of national voluntary youth organizations and other agencies who use programmes of Outdoor Education and whose members are required to make financial contributions towards the cost of participating in such activities. There is also some concern from self-employed practitioners in the outdoors who, although often highly qualified with national governing body certification, feel that, even though they may become licensed by the AALA, were they to experience an incident while instructing young people under the age of 18, they may be open to their actions being questioned (possibly under criminal rather than civil tort) in a court of law if parents brought claims of negligence against them or their company. This may be resolved in the immediate future by such practitioners simply not work-ing with any client under the legal age of consent. However, from the perspective of many educational managers and practitioners in schools or the youth service, current changes in local government boundaries and the provision for schools to opt out from local authority control, with the corresponding loss of LEA central resources, means that where proposals for involvement in adventurous outdoor activities by young people may once have been directed through a local authority inspector or adviser in Outdoor Education, fewer and fewer such positions exist. In 1994, Martin Hore, Secretary of the Outdoor Education Advisors' Panel, suggested that a quarter of the education authorities in England and Wales had no specialist advisory support in Outdoor Education (Hore, 1994).

The final word in this introductory chapter which, hopefully, will set the scene for the chapters to follow, comes appositely, from the *Proposals for Regulations and Guidance to Implement the Safety Provisions of the Activity Centres (Young Persons' Safety) Act 1995* which gives an indication of the professional nature of the vast majority of work undertaken by providers of Outdoor Education. Under 'Benefits of statutory licensing' the consultative document states:

> Analysis of available information suggests there are not many accidents in this sector, so there are few accidents which could be directly prevented by these proposals for the licensing of activity providers. School groups and voluntary organisations have had a number of accidents which are outside the scope of the proposals for statutory licensing of activity providers. (HSC, 1995)

These accidents are clarified, later in the document, as being fourteen deaths of under 18-year-olds since the early 1970s. The document goes on to state that the Health and Safety Executive's records suggest that there have been nine fatalities, in two incidents, since 1970 (Cairngorms in 1971 and Lyme Bay in 1993) which would have fallen under the scope of the proposals, and on which the document undertakes a cost-benefit assessment. The document then acknowledges that the benefits cannot just be assessed financially:

> There may be additional benefits derived by either the customers themselves or by relatives and friends of the customers in the form

of improved peace of mind as a result of knowing that the providers reached the required safety standards. These costs are not quantifiable. (*Ibid.*)

This places a considerable burden on us as leaders and teachers in the outdoors and we must not let the young people, our clients, or their parents and friends, down. Our management of outdoor programmes must be impeccable and this will require much thought and effort. However, it will be worth it, as the benefits of what we can achieve with regard to the development of young people through Outdoor Education are, likewise, unquantifiable.

2 The expedition experience: The place of the peer-group venture in Outdoor Education

Great things are done when men and mountains meet;
This is not done by jostling in the street.
William Blake, *Notebooks* (1793)

Introduction

Outdoor Education, in whatever form it is undertaken, often involves young people in living, moving and learning in the outdoors in ways that provide challenging opportunities for adventure and self-discovery. The breadth of activities which provide such opportunities is considerable. Mountainwalking, rock-climbing, caving, skiing, canoeing, sailing, rowing, horseriding and cycling all involve the components of planned travel in the outdoors and all are embraced by the overall concept of educating in the outdoors. It is not, of course, possible to crossreference every example used in this book to all forms of outdoor pursuit and, for this reason, most of the following chapters are focused on foot expeditions within a wild, mountainous, country environment. However, every process covered can be transferred among all forms of outdoor activity, and the focus on foot expeditions is not to elevate one particular activity above the others but is purely for expediency of the text.

For many young adventurers an outdoor experience, in whatever form it is undertaken, will represent the greatest challenge of their life so far. To reduce that experience to a mere completion of a number of prescribed tasks, a set number of miles to be covered, or a journey to be completed within a given time would deny the participants the opportunity to capitalize on the great potential for both personal and social development. Not everything of value we do in outdoor education can always be statistically or normatively evaluated, and the sense of pride and achievement felt by young people when their adventure is completed as a team, rather than as a collection of individuals, cannot easily be quantified, although it can, and should, be recognized.

In discussing the nature of adventure education, David Hopkins and Roger Putnam (1993) in *Personal Growth Through Adventure* identify experience as the basis of self-discovery: 'We learn about ourselves, as we learn about and interact with others and the environment in which we live' (p. 11). Developing the report of the DES Dartington Conference in October 1975, Hopkins and Putnam establish the three components of the adventure experience while emphasizing their interrelationship, namely:

- Self: For the individual participant there is the prospect that increased self-awareness and enhanced self-concept may stem from a positive response to experiences of a challenging and adventurous nature.
- Others: An expedition is a powerful medium for maximizing the potential for group development and cohesion. Indeed, successful responses to the inherent physical challenges of the venture will depend on the group's ability to forge effective underlying social structures.
- The Natural Environment: The environment provides adventure education with an arena for challenge in a physical sense, but it also has a more subtle and powerful influence. Environmental awareness grows through direct experience of the natural world and its pervading influence enlivens all that is best in Outdoor Education.

There has been increasing recognition among those working with young people of the value of these wider dimensions of the outdoor experience in promoting all-round personal and social development in areas such as self-awareness, teamwork, decision-making, environmental awareness, spiritual and aesthetic awareness, relationship-building, taking responsibility, communication skills and physical awareness. The search for this vital wider dimension, the 'Something Else' identified by The Duke of Edinburgh's Award (1996), will help to redress an apparent imbalance in the present debate over outdoor and adventure education caused by the necessary emphasis on safety and technical skills. It is well understood, however, that the wider benefits can only be experienced in ventures which have been safely and responsibly planned and prepared. Acquisition of core technical skills by participants, to at least a minimum level, prior to embarking on the venture is vitally important as they are the means whereby the personal and social aspects can be fully experienced.

So many facets of an individual's personality can be influenced by promoting these non-physical, non-technical advantages of Outdoor Education – what was, originally, in the early days of mountain centres, called 'character building' – that it is worth giving a brief overview of what is perceived to be included under 'something else', although team-building and problem-solving will be covered in more detail in later chapters.

Group dynamics

A vital part of all outdoor experiences is how the individual members of the team interact with each other, and it is often this factor of relationship-building which, above all others, determines the success or otherwise of the venture. Individuals in the group can begin to see how they fit into the team, and what they contribute to the venture. They can analyse who was leading at various intervals, or carrying the map, or chatting, or joking, or moaning, or eating, and from this can identify and discuss which member of the team was undertaking which role, such as who seemed to be the natural group leader, or the morale booster or who was inclined to be the navigator. All roles within the group are equally valuable and mutually complementary. It is often hard for the young person wrapped up in the experience to acknowledge it happening. However, through watching and discussing what each individual does, they can, perhaps, begin to form an impression of what the exact role is that each performs within the group.

Each member of the group has a role, whether this is consciously acknowledged or not. Are individual members of the group interchangeable? Could the 'navigator' become the 'motivator' and vice versa? Or is it the unique personality of each individual which influences which role within the group they perform? By identifying their own strengths as individuals and through recognizing the strengths of others, young people may begin to see the importance of a complementary team and that some roles may, from necessity, be more inclined towards leadership.

The concept of leadership

It may well be the case within a group of young people involved on an outdoor experience, especially if they are undertaking any form of peer group expedition or journey, that the 'leadership' may rotate around the members of the group depending upon which task has to be performed. Considerable research has been done on the subject of leadership and John Adair's (1988a) three 'areas of need' are often used to identify the functions that leaders should perform: Awareness (of what is going on in the group); Understanding (knowing that a particular function is required); Skill (to do it well enough to be effective).

Are these membership or leadership functions? Should every member of the group or team perform these functions or just the 'leader'? Adair makes the point that it is often better to talk about 'leadership' rather 'leaders' and that leadership resides in the functions not in a person. Therefore, the group could share leadership among themselves and leadership would pass from person to person. Can the young people recognize when and how the 'leadership' of the group was passed from one individual member to another and which particular task was being carried out at the time? Does the group feel the need to have a nominated 'leader' for certain tasks outside the actual venture itself? Could the group decide to have a different nominated 'leader' for each day of the expedition? Should this involve functions such as ensuring that the group were out of bed on time every morning, and that the campsite was free of litter? Or are these tasks that the group should perform among themselves as a matter of course?

How do the group feel about having a leader in case they have an accident on the hill? What happens if it is the leader (in the traditional sense) who is the casualty and cannot, therefore, exercise their role? Should every member of the group be capable of assuming 'leadership' of the group at any given time? Has a natural leader emerged during the period of training? Does the group need a leader after the venture to ensure that aspects of the post-venture stage, such as the developing of photographs, are completed?

Team-building

Once we have encouraged individual members of the group to think about how they see themselves, and how they feel others perceive them, we can introduce the notion of the building and performance of a team. The expedition group, to successfully complete the task in hand, should perform as a team. They come together at the beginning of the planning stage of the venture as a collection of individuals but, through the process of training and preparation, they gradually form together as a cohesive unit.

Problem-solving

Another interesting aspect of the group's mental approach to the venture is how they respond to critical moments on the expedition when they are required to confront a very real problem. All sorts of events, throughout the duration of the venture, will require the group to exercise their collective problem-solving abilities. At each point there will, naturally, be several different opinions from different members of the group as to how exactly to deal with the problem. How does the group decide which action to take? Is there fair and 'democratic' debate, or is a more random and arbitrary decision made? Does the quality of debate change at different stages of the venture, for example, when the weather is bad, or when group members are feeling tired and irritable?

Can we introduce to the group the notion of 'brainstorming' as a way of solving problems which arise *en route*? Brainstorming works by encouraging people to deliberately suspend judgement, to refrain from criticism and to think of as many ideas – or solutions to the problem – as possible. Instead of attempting to immediately identify the correct solution to every problem (which path to take, where to site the tent at an overnight stop, etc.) should we encourage all members of the group to throw in as many ideas or suggestions as possible. Each of these can then be discussed, on its own merits, by the group and accepted or rejected until the best possible solution is found. This is an especially useful technique to use when navigating in poor visibility, as a few minutes spent contemplating all the possible alternatives could well save a great deal of time and effort which could be wasted following the wrong path only to say, when you discover you have been going the wrong way, 'if only we had thought of that earlier!'

Environmental awareness

The environment, especially the wilderness of open and wild country and the majestic splendour of the mountains, can certainly have an inspirational effect on people; we only have to look at the number of paintings, photographs, poems, plays, novels and films which have used the outdoors as a natural backdrop, to realize the truth in this. But how do we convey this to young people who will not have the time to attempt anything of great inspirational depth? The outdoors can have an immense effect on shaping our own individual philosophy to life, as well as making us think about wider environmental issues and the world in general. The impact of sitting on top of an inspiring mountain peak or summit is often very great, both for young people who do not get the opportunity very often, as well as those who spend a large amount of time in such landscapes. Through this experience, young people can begin to appreciate the environment as a precious natural resource. The environment provides us with an area for challenging adventure, but it also has a more subtle and powerful influence. This is more difficult to recognize or express, but learning to be at one with nature, through our understanding of it and ourselves, is an important ingredient of any outdoor experience.

The feeling of how small we are in comparison to the mountains is a common one, often arising in expedition reports, and certainly prompts young people to consider the natural environment, realize what a precious resource it is, and how we should do all we can to protect it. This, perhaps, is how we can incorporate philosophical reflection and awareness into our ventures, by considering the wider issues and long-term results of our actions. The very fact that we have walked across a wilderness or moor may mean that, through the cumulative damaging effects of our actions, and other groups like us, on the environment, future generations may not have the same experience. By looking at wide, open-ended, questions which do not, by their definition, have a finite answer, we may encourage young people to think on a broader philosophical base.

Evaluating the experience

It is important that, in addition to providing a valuable outdoor experience, we encourage young people to understand the personal impact of the projects they undertake. The experience

31

should offer ways in which young people can – possibly for the first time ever – offer some meaningful evaluations of themselves rather than having someone else do it. The process is an important one to learn, and is a valid learning experience. It is very interesting for a leader or teacher to hear how the group themselves felt that they had performed, rather than those in positions of authority expressing an opinion as to the performance. The group members impressions are of vital importance and an integral part of the total experience of the venture. They provide a valuable snapshot of an altogether bigger picture.

Any outdoor experience may be the most challenging undertaking that a young person has attempted so far in their lives, and may remain one of the most demanding. It should certainly be a 'treasured memory' as inferred above, one which remain with the young person for a long time to come – what Abraham Maslow (1968) calls a 'peak experience'.

Michael Paffard in his book *Inglorious Wordsworths*, gives numerous examples in their own words of young people's reactions to forms of outdoor peak experiences. One, especially, is appropriate:

> As we approached Pen-y-Gwryd at the head of Nantygwryd, I was suddenly awe-struck. Dusk was beginning to fade as we turned S.W. down the valley. On the opposite side, as we looked into the setting sun, was the Horseshoe, the great corrie with its waterfalls tumbling down into the valley below and Snowdon itself towering above. Looking down the valley we could see Llyn Dinas and Llyn Gwynant glistening silver below the trees and steep valley sides.
> I find my feelings beyond description – all I can say is that it made me 'feel good inside', good to be alive. This feeling stayed with me all that week. Waking up in the morning in our tent quite high up the valley side and walking through the dewy grass to wash in a tiny stream, we could hear the cattle lowing on the valley floor.
> It would echo eerily up the silent valley. We felt free and at peace. I still look back on that week and have a strange tingling in my blood. (Paffard, 1973)

We should, surely, encourage young people to review and reflect on their venture in these terms, to look for the inspirational moments or the overall effect of the trip. An important aspect of each person's personality is the ability to express themselves and the venture will be, for many, the first 'real lived' experience that they can relate to in these terms. It is, of course, unrealistic to expect that every young person will be able to record their feelings and emotions poetically or through fine prose; neither will they all be able to capture those special moments through works of art. But they will all be able to recognize that such moments have occurred and, thus, will have taken their personal and social development one stage further.

Outdoor Education can provide a turning-point in a young person's development and we must encourage them to make the most of the experience. We should maximize the potential of our young people by enabling them to take part in an exciting adventurous experience which stretches every aspect of their personality. We should not allow them to feel, in years to come, that they have had the experience, but missed the meaning!

A personal perspective

More a way of life!

'Our expedition was great, I don't ever want to do it again!' As we have seen in Chapter 1, many youth organizations and agencies include some form of outdoor journeying activity in their structured training programmes, and the above quote is often the reaction of many young people on completing the experience. Teenagers often view a planned foot venture which involves several nights spent camping in the remoter, wild, country areas of the UK as something to be done in a similar superficial way to tourists who 'do' Europe. They seldom, unfortunately, view it as a stimulus and stepping-stone for a way of life or a potential lifetime's involvement and enjoyment in the countryside.

It has already been stated that many educational and youth work providers agree that Outdoor Education is a vehicle for the promotion of personal and social development in young people, and journeying or expeditioning in open countryside is a vital part of that, especially if the participants have been responsible for planning their own routes and have completed the venture as a self-led peer group expedition. Most would also agree that such undertakings provide a challenge, but is that challenge enough? Ventures may be physically demanding and mentally tiring, but are they intellectually stimulating? Do they put the 'education' in Outdoor Education?

Rather than merely passing through the countryside, are young people encouraged to question and investigate the environment by asking How? Why? What? and When? instead of conforming to the 'heads down – miles covered' philosophy by completing a certain preset distance in a given amount of time. This is, arguably, little different from walking on a treadmill for a few days, carrying a heavy pack, with the occasional bucket of water being thrown over them for good measure! Do young people set out to undertake specific, preplanned objectives along their journey to find out information which, being hopefully new to them, will teach them more about the land through which they may previously have walked 'unseeing', thus adding to the overall experience of the venture.

Having a purpose

It is hard to think of a major expedition, the sort of classic expedition which captures the public's imagination and is the stuff of which television documentaries are made, which has not had specific objectives, aims and purpose – whether this is to discover new species of flora or fauna, to map a previously uncharted river or cave system, or to retrace historical journeys in reconstructed craft to see if they could have been completed as ancient myths and legends would have us believe. All such major expeditions usually begin from the How? Why? What?

and When? during what, as we shall see later, is termed the concept stage of the venture, and are then planned around the objectives. This is especially true of those fortunate, high-profile adventures which attract commercial sponsorship from large companies who are unlikely to invest in ventures whose prime motive appears to be simply for the participants to have a good time.

Some, of course, would point to the 'because it was there' rationale, the desire to be first to conquer an unclimbed peak or the first to walk across a certain area of hostile terrain. I maintain that, when analysed simplistically, this motivation boils down to simply seeing if it can be done. I would argue that this option is only, in reality, open to personalities fortunate or well-known enough to be able to visit the diminishing number of remote corners of the world that have never been conquered. It is hard, for example, for a group of Scouts to 'see if it can be done' on a four-day visit to the Lake District, especially when confronted with the queue of holiday-makers on Helvellyn on a Bank Holiday Sunday.

I would concede that the 'can it be done?' syndrome has a place and value with certain young people if subtly amended to become 'can we do it?' By this change of emphasis – to the personal – the adventure becomes, in many respects, an exploration of the self and we have all seen the reactions of young people who, ten feet tall with pride, tell that they never thought they were going to be able to complete their journey, climb or abseil. As long as this approach is not taken to extremes, the challenge of completing a physically demanding journey or an emotionally demanding activity – if appropriate to the individual concerned – can provide more of a stimulus and ongoing motivator to certain personalities than any amount of observing along the way.

I would, however, maintain that having a purpose for the expedition is a fundamental criteria for any venture and, as such, should be so inextricably linked with all stages of the planning, practice and preparation for the journey that all ventures become, in effect, explorations, as distinct from expeditions. This distinction in terms has been described by A. P. Lowery as 'an expedition is a journey with a purpose, whilst an exploration is a purpose with a journey' (The Duke of Edinburgh's Award, 1981, p. 9).

A *historical perspective*

To see just how closely the purpose should be linked to all ventures, it may be useful to take a historical perspective. It is generally acknowledged that the golden age of exploration and discovery, at least in European terms, was during the period between 1492 and the late 1700s. This was the era when great explorers such as Columbus and Vasco da Gama set sail to discover new worlds when many were not even completely sure about the old one!

These first explorers set out to see if the world really was flat, testing themselves, their equipment and their navigation to the limits. This demonstrates how important the purpose is to the planning. Just how much food and fresh water do you take if you do not know how far you will go or how long the expedition will last? What actually drove these expeditions to leave the safety of their sheltered coastal trade routes for unmapped oceans, especially as they did not know (other than from folk tales of far-off lands) exactly what, if anything, they would find or whether they would ever return. Since they did return, bringing back stories, treasures and imports such as tobacco and potatoes from the New World, and subsequent generations have gone on to discover and map the entire globe, does this mean that modern exploration is impossible? Has everything been done?

It is interesting that what could be termed the next golden age of discovery owes much to the descendants of the New World which Columbus colonized when, in the 1960s America set out to journey to the Moon. Like the early explorations, the moon probes were planned to the smallest details and, although the

Apollo missions had the advantage of knowing where they were going and how far away it was, they still did not know exactly what they would find. What would they have done if the Moon really had been made of cheese? This again illustrates, although from a reverse perspective, just how closely the objectives are linked with the actual expedition, as the journey was essential to find out the answer to the aims. We can see that, in all ventures, the purpose is vital to the journey and, in turn, the journey is vital to complete the purpose.

Setting sail towards the edge of the earth, and sailing over the horizon, is the same quantum leap in mankind's attitude towards, and understanding of, our environment – in the broadest sense – as the crew of the Apollo mission circumnavigating the Moon and becoming the first human beings, ever, to lose sight of the earth. The very first human beings in history to actually loose sight of the planet on which every other human has been born and has lived. This, to me, is a truly awe-inspiring concept. The thought of humanity exploring the very outer edges of our knowledge should inspire young people to explore the limits of their personal experiences, and what better way than by journeying through their own endeavours? As the saying goes, 'travel broadens the mind', yet how can we instil the same sense of wonder into today's urban young people, with the current 'street corner' culture who know that the world is not flat and who do not have the $400 billion necessary to reach the Moon and, often, do not even have the 40p bus fare to travel out of town?

I would argue that the concept of exploration is an attitude of mind rather than merely going through the largely mechanical process of gathering specimens along the route to stick into the report of your expedition. The ancient Chinese believed the journey to be more important than the destination, as did Robert Louis Stevenson (1850–94) when, in *El Dorado*, he suggested that 'To travel hopefully is a better thing than to arrive.' Some people appear to go through life as if on a route march – very target and time-scale orientated where the destination – such as career objectives and material acquisitions – is all-important. Others explore their way through life, always ready to learn something new for the sheer sake of it or to alter direction if something attracts their interest and attention. Although this is not to imply that one is better than the other, it does illustrate that different people have differing values and methods of operating which, when applied to Outdoor Education with modern young people, should be taken into account so that each individual achieves the maximum possible benefit out of the total experience of the venture.

An expedition not a route march

I believe that young people should, therefore, be encouraged into exploring, rather than just travelling, and to journey with their eyes, ears and noses – not to mention their minds – firmly open so that their senses can experience all facets of venturing in new environments. As Malcolm S. Forbes is credited with saying: 'Education's purpose is to replace an empty mind with an open one.' Journeying in this way should become a complete sensual, and possibly even sensitive, experience with all the distinctive sights, sounds and smells of the area being absorbed, subconsciously if not consciously. This is what, I believe, makes Outdoor Education truly worthwhile in a 'whole person' sense, and even good for the soul. Those of us who are fortunate enough to have spent significant amounts of time walking, climbing, canoeing, caving, cycling or sailing in various parts of the world have learnt, gradually, that it is often being in the remote, unspoilt areas which is important and enjoyable rather than actually participating in the activity which has either got you there – as in cycling or mountainwalking – or that you have journeyed there to undertake – as in caving or rock-climbing. Being there is often enough! With the benefit of the hindsight of experience, climbers are often happy to 'fester' at the foot of crags and walkers happy to 'rest a while' by a lake or on a summit and watch the world pass by. As the old saying goes: 'Sometimes I sits and thinks; sometimes I just sits!'

An attitude of mind

If this attitude of mind – of travelling with receptive senses – is encouraged in young people from their first outings to the fringes of the urban areas in which they live and is then developed through whatever programme of Outdoor Education, formal or informal, in which they are involved, it will become second nature to question and discover what is around them. Exploring will not, then, be seen as a separate activity reserved for the field trip, but an additional component in all aspects of life.

In this way young people will still be able, if they so wish, to opt to simply take part in the adventurous activities to which they have been introduced, but will have the additional benefit of participating in such activities while walking and talking about the countryside in which they find themselves. They will gradually begin to investigate, albeit superficially, things which they encounter or pass on their wanderings. Through this process, young people can become historical and geographical detectives as the How? Why? What? and When? will not only be vital to the purpose of their venture, but it will also become important to the execution of the journey as the participants will, hopefully, begin to wonder: 'How did this get here? When was it built? Why is this valley the shape it is?' Thus, as stated earlier, it will become impossible to travel or undertake an adventurous activity without it becoming exploratory. After all, to take part in the apparent simply physical activity of rock-climbing, the young person will, at least, need a basic knowledge of geology and rock formations to ensure that the rock-face on which they are climbing will not, literally, come apart in their hands!

The urban explorer

This open-minded approach to the environment is not restricted solely to the minimal number of days that each individual young person is able to devote to outdoor adventurous activities. How many of the vast majority of the population who live or work within the centres of our large cities ever truly notice their surroundings? How many people, for example, ever look up in the streets of the towns and cities in which they live? Much of the business and shopping centres of our old-established urban conurbations have fascinating stories to tell the archaeological detective. Above the plastic fascias of shop fronts, which now seem identical in every medium-sized town in the country, there are generations of interesting buildings and features. All these, like settlements of the ancient Britons, have been built upon by successive generations down the years and the modern sociologist could tell a great deal about the fashions and trends of modern culture by looking at the layers hidden behind shop-fronts – this decade's Next covering our grandparent's Home and Colonial. As W. G. Hoskins reportedly observed: 'One cannot understand the English landscape, town or country, or savour it to the full, apprehend all its wonderful variety, without going back to the history that lies behind it.' People seldom stop to look above the initial façade and veneer of the shops as they are always in too much of a hurry to scratch below the surface. Too concerned with getting to their destination, in reaching their objective, in covering the distance to work in the five minutes too little time which they have allowed themselves.

Why do we seem to encourage our young people to treat the outdoors in the same way that we lead most of our lives and to transfer the 'heads down and rush' approach, intact, to the peace and tranquillity of the countryside and the possible calming effects of a journey through it?

Doing their own thing

Studying the architecture of urban conurbations on the way to work obviously has little place in Outdoor Education, as we currently understand it, where the concept of adventure, challenge and, possibly, remoteness, is vital. However, the parallel illustrates, I believe, how important it is to have a preconceived and suitably focused purpose, and resulting structure, to every venture and journey into the countryside.

But how do we initiate, and then sustain, this exploratory approach in young people who, in the age of *Life on Earth* documentaries and professional explorers walking to both poles, believe that everything has been done? Indeed, the very nature of adventurous explorations has changed considerably in a less than a century; while Victorian explorers set off to discover new tribes or map uncharted continents, modern-day explorers are more likely to be attempting to be the first person to walk unaided to both poles, the first person to climb the highest mountain in each of the continents or to circumnavigate the world in a balloon. As Matthew Bond (1997) said, rather cynically:

> Long gone are the days when 'because it's there' was sufficient excuse to get the rucksack out of the attic. What the modern multimedia explorer needs is an idea sufficiently offbeat to get television interested and perhaps a publisher or two.

This theme was nicely picked up on the eve of Richard Branson's attempted record-breaking balloon expedition, by Bill Frost (1997) who wrote that Richard Branson had

> restored our love for conquest and the thrill of danger with a plot worthy of Jules Verne. With no new lands to discover, peaks to conquer or ocean depths to plumb, there was only one option left – onwards and upwards in the flight path of Phileas Fogg.

We cannot, therefore, expect every group of young people on short-term ventures to make discoveries or conquests of earth-shattering proportions. University research departments, television film crews, full-time natural history writers and environmental organizations, not to mention multinational industrial, mining and pharmaceutical concerns, have long-term interests and investments in trying to uncover more information about the world in which we live, and their resources are far beyond the interested and enthusiastic amateur who is usually responsible for introducing young people to adventurous out-door activities. We can, however, encourage and help our young people to discover something which is new or original to themselves.

By having a purpose which is planned into the outing from the initial stages of preparation, we can make the venture a long-term experience rather than a short-term wonder. Many people today crave instant adventure. Activity and adventure holidays provide immediate thrills for the young. Any one of us could climb Mont Blanc or the Matterhorn tomorrow, if we had the money, with a multitude of tour operators and many have paid to join expeditions to Everest or other exotic locations. But surely an expedition should be more than just short-term excitement? The venture should be a whole experience, not a fairground ride. True Outdoor Education should not be something which young people are 'packed-off' on for the convenience of their parents or leaders. Young people must be empowered to take responsibility for their own experiences. The outing should be planned by the group, for the group – the adventure belongs to them!

Remember the early explorers of the Middle Ages. They had no cameras, newspapers or other media to document and record every moment of their exploits and, as such, retained a sort of editorial control over their discoveries, mounting exhibitions and paintings of new continents and exotic fruits and plants on their return home. What a contrast to Neil Armstrong who, on 21 July 1969, became the first man to set foot on the Moon watched live, through the wonders of modern technology, by over 723 million people world-wide. The achievement is almost dimmed by the fact that we all share it. What, exactly, was the giant technological breakthrough, the fact that a man had walked on the Moon, or that so many people watched it happen 'live'? The over-exposure of media attention can possibly make us blasé about the actual event. The first steps on the Moon belong, in effect, to a whole generation of television viewers!

Let us ensure that our young people assist in the planning of their own excursions into the outdoors, prepare the purpose and method of recording their adventure. Let them practise what they will do and how they will do it, learning new skills and techniques along the way. Encourage them on their training and preparatory sessions to walk and talk, to stop and question. So long as they have allowed for flexibility in their planning, young people should stop every once in a while to sit and look, to eat their packed lunch in isolated splendour or to discover more about the environment. Even better if they can plan and make their own investigatory equipment, and we can encourage them to count or measure using simple, homemade equipment or by adapting that which they have with them. In this way, true *Blue Peter* style, tent poles become impromptu measuring sticks or sighting poles and a piece of string and four tent pegs become a square 'quadrat' for counting the distribution of plants in a given area.

This whole approach of impelling young people into the experience can be taken a stage further. Think of the feeling of achievement which young people would experience through completing a venture wearing a jacket or using a pair of gaiters that they had designed and made themselves, to their individual specification, or surviving for several nights in a tent which they, as a group, had planned, modified and then constructed – having found suppliers of the appropriate materials – and then field tested. All this cannot, of course, be done in the minibus on the way up the motorway and, thus, requires possibly more initial input from leaders and trainers. But do we not owe it to our young people to aim for the total experience and not just the superficial target!

The theory into practice?

Can this personal philosophy be made a reality? Can the theory outlined above be put into practice within the increasingly full educational curriculum or youth service programme? Do young people want to be involved? That is all down to us as leaders. It will not be easy, but the following chapters may offer advice which enables the process to be planned from the outset and delivered professionally. If we accept the challenge of providing real and meaningful education outdoors, I'm sure that the young people will accept the challenge of participation.

3 Is fear the key? Exploring the concept of risk in Outdoor Education

Believe me!
The secret of reaping the greatest fruitfulness and the greatest
enjoyment from life is to live dangerously!
                        Friedrich Nietzsche (1844–1900)

Introduction

The 1995 revision of the National Curriculum required schools
to teach the skills of hazard recognition, risk assessment and
risk management. This was an important development, and one
where Outdoor Education has much to contribute, as risk, like
love, to paraphrase the pop song, is all around. Everywhere we
go and everything we do involves an element of risk. We cannot
escape it. With today's frenetic lifestyles people of all ages face
risks greater than they have ever done before. But what exactly
do we mean by risk? Is it danger? The chance of disaster or loss?
Putting something in jeopardy? Taking a chance? Being in a
hazardous situation?

What is risk?

The definition of risk will provoke varying reactions across
different professions. Medical practitioners may be interested
in the biological changes which take place in the body when
imminent danger makes the adrenal medulla produce the hor-
mones adrenaline and noradrenaline which mobilizes the body
by, among other things, raising the metabolic rate and diverting

blood flow from the skin, stomach and intestines to the limbs, thus making us ready for the so-called 'fright, flight or fight'. Psychologists may focus on the motivation behind some people's continual pursuit of the thrill factor, fear and an adrenaline rush through participation in high risk sports, while other folk are content to curl up by the fire with a book. Factory inspectors may be concerned with identifying potentially dangerous situations which could possibly happen at any stage of industrial processes and in putting protocols in place to prevent accidents occurring. Sociologists may be interested in highly dangerous risk-taking phenomena such as subway surfing and the place it has in modern youth culture, while marketing professionals may see an opportunity to adopt such exciting images for mainstream advertising such as in the Benetton advertisements showing the Brazilian barrio boys in Rio de Janerio riding the roofs of urban trains or Reebok sports shoes featuring bungee-jumpers in their TV advertisements. Copywriters may see the ability of by-lines such as 'designed for the pursuit of fear' to attract readers' attention in magazines, while philosophers may ponder on the value of life without risk. Even in education, primary teachers may focus on potential risks for their pupils such as crossing the road or talking to strangers, and colleagues in the secondary sector may be concerned with risks from personal, social and health education issues such as drugs and sex.

The expression 'young people at risk' is now widely used within education, youth work and the social services to categorize those who, through their social circumstances, are in danger of being corrupted or abused by external influences into anti-social activities or behaviour. This is not, however, the type of risk which this chapter is addressing. In outdoor terms, risk is accepted as being the potential for danger or the chances of injury or death occurring if something were to go wrong as a direct result of participation in challenging outdoor pursuits; the situations when, as Colin Mortlock (1984) so succinctly suggests, adventure becomes misadventure. Indeed, the very terminology surrounding Outdoor Education implies a definite acceptance of risk. As the *Oxford Reference Dictionary* (1986) states, 'adventure' is 'an unusual and exciting or dangerous experience; a willingness to take risks' and a 'venture', often used to describe expeditions, is defined as 'an undertaking that involves risk'. Our task is to minimize the risk and the accepted definition of adventure in the outdoors is, therefore, very much related to safety. As the UK Mountain Training Board state in *National Guidelines*:

> Challenge and adventure are never free of risk. Learning to have regard for the safety of oneself and others is an aspect of the personal development of participants to which good instruction and leadership will make an important contribution. However, there must always be an acceptable framework of safety. (UKMTB, 1995, p. 14)

The concept of excitement and adventure within a framework of safety is an important factor in many peoples' lives, whether, at one extreme, they actively seek it out through participation in sports and activities with high levels of controlled risk, or whether they are more content with the occasional, short-term thrill of a fairground ride. Quentin Crisp writing from the USA, once said that life had become so sanitized that being afraid was the last remaining emotion available to us. He suggested that this was why so many people watched thriller films at the cinema, because 'American urban life has become so safe, so bland, we have to go to the movies to feel anything' (Crisp, 1996). This notion was substantiated recently when Alton Towers, the theme park, commissioned a psychologist, David Lewis, to investigate what the public craved from the rides on offer. He found that adventure was high on the list and believes that this is because 'in an attempt to guarantee safety, our culture has eliminated risk' (Lewis, 1994, p. 7). Alton Towers cannot, of course, offer rides which incur real, or actual, risk. They must offer perceived risk and the thrill of hurtling around an aerial track in as near total safety as is possible.

47

A risk threshold

It may be, of course, that not only is the literal definition of risk different between professions, but that the perception of risk differs between individuals. In the same way that everyone has differing levels of tolerance to pain, do we each have our own, highly individual, risk threshold? It cannot be that it is only because of experience and conditioning, or the potential for financial reward, that some people are willing to subject themselves to risk on a daily basis. All of us have our own unique sense of humour, phobias and tastes, and there is no reason to assume that this does not equally apply to the perception of risk. A Royal Society study group report raises this issue when considering the acceptability of risk, and suggests that we are all affected in our individual acceptance of risk by external factors: 'People are subjected to, and apparently accept, very different levels of risk, depending on their occupation, their life-style, their hobbies and, above all, their age' (Royal Society, 1983, p. 157). This is a view shared by John Adams, who suggests that we all come equipped with 'risk thermostats' and, based on a model originally devised by Gerald Wilde, illustrates this in diagrammatic form where 'individual risk-taking decisions represent a balancing act in which perceptions of risk are weighed against propensity to take risk' (Adams, 1995, p. ix). If this is so, we must ensure that, when dealing with groups of young people, we are not pushing some over their own personal boundaries of risk into unacceptable activities simply because we, or the rest of the group, do not share the same anxieties or have the same threshold or tolerance to risk and perceived danger. In the publication *Outdoor Education – Safety and Good Practice* (1988) representatives from the many outdoor associations and committees who compiled the text, stated in a section entitled 'Accommodating Risk' that 'Reference to the risk of psychological harm should not be overlooked. This can be present for some people in the most innocuous situations' (p. 27). The responsible teacher or leader should be very aware of such dilemmas.

It may also be the case that our individual understanding and awareness of danger, and our personal ability to accept risk, changes as we develop, age and mature. Certainly, interesting work has been carried out by the Health Education Unit in the School of Education at the University of Southampton whose observations of children's behaviour indicates a progressive maturing of risk perception. Jenny McWhirter (1996), who heads a project which aims to asses how much risk management advice children understand and to help teachers identify the most appropriate methods of putting information across, has found, for example, that young children will protect themselves from a fire in their room by 'hiding' under the bedclothes, whereas older children understand that they should try to escape.

This progressive, developmental, understanding of risk by young people is, naturally, of great interest and importance to those of us involved in Outdoor Education. The 'risk' appreciated by a 10-year-old child on a primary school residential visit may be the fact of being away from parents and the family home for a number of evenings. We do not need to increase the burden of risk, whether real or imaginary, by the activities the teacher and school offer during the trip, for the venture to be extremely meaningful in terms of broadening the child's horizons. However, this may be significantly different for a 16-year-old on a residential activities week, to whom the prospect of adventure, potential danger and overcoming perceived risk are important ingredients.

This developmental approach to the understanding of risk is especially relevant to those of us dealing with adolescents, as the ability of teenagers to recognize risk, and their aptitude for approaching it sensibly and rationally, will be maturing and we can provide experiences which promote this facet of their personalities. However, we must be aware of an apparent contradiction to this stance in what has been termed the 'window of immortality' where people in their late teens and early twenties feel that nothing drastic can happen to them as they have their whole lives ahead of them, although this may, of course, be more to do with how they approach challenge and adventure rather than how they perceive risk.

Excitement and adventure in youth

I firmly believe that if young people cannot get their excitement and adventure in ways which are acceptable to society, they will get them in ways which are socially unacceptable. We only need to look at recent youth 'cult' activities such as tagging (spray painting names in as many places as possible, the more dangerous and difficult the surface – such as the front of bridges or the side of trains – the more peer status received) graffiti painting (where gangs will try and outdo each other for the complexity, colour and position of their creations) and, at the higher extremes, subway surfing (where youngsters climb on to the top of moving trains and stand up in a highly dangerous imitation of surfers riding waves, often with fatal results), car theft and joy-riding. These activities not only carry their own innate physical risks, and associated thrills, but, of course, have the added excitement of breaking the law and the risk of being arrested.

This need for excitement and the establishing of their own culture among the young can also be seen in more acceptable activities, such as the imported 'laid back' Californian image associated with skateboarding, BMX biking, roller hockey and snowboarding, where particular clothing, attitude, lifestyle and a general contempt of anyone not enmeshed into their particular activity are all recurrent themes. This extends, of course, into all aspects of modern adolescence and Sir Michael Rutter and Professor David Smith, in their report *Psychosocial Disorders in Young People* (1996) identify the growth of 'an isolated youth culture' since World War II. The report states that:

> . . . over the course of the twentieth century, the meaning of adolescence as a development period has changed a great deal. To begin with, there have been major alterations in the social construction of adolescence. These are evident in legislation on

compulsory education, in the laws differentiating juveniles from adult offenders, and in legal restrictions on the employment of juveniles. However, they are also apparent in the mass youth consumer market (in clothes, music and entertainment) that came into being after the Second World War, and in the growth of youth cultures. (Smith and Rutter, 1996, p. 68)

It is also relevant to remember the importance of language among such groupings, and a characteristic of all of the street culture activities mentioned above is that they develop their own words, slang and code of communication. This, of course, is nothing new and examples can be found among London's apprentice boys in the 1600s. More recently, Mungham and Pearson, in *Working Class Youth Culture* (1976), argued that certain adolescents chose to avoid establishment terms and to maintain a separate identity and argot, and the considerable body of research that has been undertaken into the development and history of popular and youth culture only confirms that this has always been so.

However, it is at these fringes of street culture that we as Outdoor Education practitioners can often find common ground with young people in search of adventure, and this is one reason why outdoor programmes are so often and effectively used with young offenders or groups from the social services. The risk, excitement and thrill of outdoor pursuits such as rock-climbing, canoeing, surfing, mountaineering, skiing, or caving along with their associated individualized terminology and clothing, as well as being – to the general public – rather 'alternative' activities, can be very attractive to young people wishing to set themselves apart, in their eyes at least, from their 'boring' parents, teachers and surroundings, and achieve something in their own terms. These sentiments are echoed by Lord Hunt, the editor of *In Search of Adventure* who stated:

We do not claim that physical activities in a natural environment provide, by themselves, a panacea for our social problems. Much is being done, through changes in the education system, job training schemes and provision for other leisure activities and skills. These are all important aspects of preparing for adult life. But with ever-advancing technology, opportunities for less-skilled work are becoming fewer. For many people there is more leisure. It is vitally important to encourage all young people, whether or not they are fully employed, to be enterprising and adventurous, and to help them – through education, training and leisure provision – to widen their interests. (Hunt, 1989, p. 12)

Hunt recognizes here, as we saw in Chapter 1, a broader conceptualization of the role of education; not just jobs and training, but education for life. This factor was recognized by the consultative document *Proposals for Regulations and Guidance to Implement the Safety Provisions of the Activity Centres (Young Persons' Safety) Act 1995*, referred to earlier, which acknowledged that:

There is widespread recognition that some degree of risk is unavoidable, if these activities are to accomplish their essential purpose. The activities allow young people to develop by meeting challenges they do not necessarily face every day and to experience a sense of achievement in overcoming them. (HSC, 1995, p. 5)

The fact that outdoor activities could also be dangerous is often an added inducement to teenagers 'looking for kicks' and all too often tempted towards anti-social forms of excitement. The element of the unknown adds significantly to the challenge of adventurous activities and, therefore, offers greater opportunity for meaningful personal growth on the part of the young people. In fact, it is the reconciling of challenge and safety which makes participation in Outdoor Education such a valuable tool for promoting excitement, coupled with a sense of responsibility, and the risk awareness required by the National Curriculum, in the young. As Eric Langmuir is often quoted as observing: To say that we can achieve balance between challenge and adventure is wishful thinking. The best we can hope for is an uneasy truce. This means that the outdoor educator must accept the constant vigilance necessary to make the activity sufficiently adventurous to challenge and excite the young, but within a controlled framework which protects, as a paramount objective, their well-being.

Real risk or perceived risk

This controlled framework means, in effect, that a priority is the identification of risk and the introduction of mechanisms to ensure that it is contained at acceptable levels, while allowing the impression, to the young people participating in the activity, that risk – and the associated adventure, challenge and excitement – remains. This juggling of real and perceived risk requires constant vigilance on behalf of the leader. Even in situations where the true risk is minimized through safety procedures and equipment (although the perceived risk, to the young people, may be significant), such as carefully supervised abseiling, the real, or actual risk still remains, often with potentially severe consequences. This real versus perceived balance is important not only to ensure the safety of the young people, but to maximize the value and worth they obtain from involvement in outdoor activities if we are serious about the positive developmental aspects of our programmes. This aspect is nicely illustrated by the reaction of 13-year-old Lee Sykes, a wheelchair-bound juvenile arthritis sufferer, who attended an activities week at the Calvert Trust in the Lake District which specializes in programmes for disabled youngsters. Lee is quoted as saying 'Abseiling is exciting and scary, it's brilliant. It's usually for people who can walk, so for wheelchairs it's really challenging' (Owens, 1996). Lee felt here that he was truly at risk, although it will be obvious to any educationalist that the Calvert Trust would have taken every possible safety precaution before exposing him to the activity. However, it is the fact that, in a very real way, he pushed forward his boundaries of fear and adventure and what he felt was possible which is of importance and lasting value. Asubi Iwerrah (1996), a youth worker from Southwark, summarized this reaction very nicely when he stated at a recent conference that 'life is definitely not a spectator sport' which is also a recurrent theme found, at the other end of the adventure spectrum, in the journals of great explorers. Sir Francis Chichester, who sailed single-handedly around the world in 1967, stated in the journal he wrote while at sea that 'It is only by submitting to trial that an individual can learn to know what is in him. Most of us are content to pass over the surface of life. We have not.'

If risk were to be eliminated completely from Outdoor Education, this sense of achievement felt by participants may very well be lost. It is exactly the concept of having ultimate control over one's destiny, with very real consequences, which makes what we do so valuable. The thrills may remain if we were to reduce abseiling to a totally safe 'virtual reality' or fairground experience, but would young people like Lee derive the same benefits in terms of their personal and social development? So, if we are to accept that the activity, with its associated risks, is educationally valuable, what can be done to consider the notion of risk realistically, to compare risk in Outdoor Education against other activities, and to find methodologies for reducing it to acceptable levels?

A statistical comparison of risk in relation to other sports

Although most people would not be able to prove it empirically, or to produce facts to illustrate the point, it would not be contentious to state that conventional wisdom dictates that some activities are perceived to be more dangerous than others. We all, instinctively, rely on our feelings, perceptions, knowledge and past experience as to what we consider to be safe. This may be sufficient if our actions only affect ourselves, but it is not adequate if our actions and decisions affect the well-being of others.

If we assume that the most common definition of risk is the likelihood of injury or death, we can compare statistics between outdoor activities and other sports. If one were to ask which sport caused more deaths, rock-climbing or badminton, many people would select rock-climbing based on their perception of climbers hanging like insects off sheer rock-faces. In fact, figures available from the Office of Population Censuses and Surveys (OPCS, 1992), shows that rock-climbing and badminton both had one fatality registered during the year 1992. The survey does not, however, make any reference to, or comparison with, any differences in the number of participants in each sport, or the number of hours of participation providing statistics on, say, the number of fatalities per 1,000 hours of person participation. The natural reaction is, of course, that the person killed rock-climbing fell to their death as a direct result of participating in the sport, while the person who died while playing badminton suffered a heart attack, or similar, during the game which could have happened anywhere and was not, in itself, a direct result of the sport. However, OPCS (1992, p. 1) states that the figures are 'generated only when a coroner mentions a sporting or leisure activity with the cause of death, or from supplementary information supplied at death registration'. The survey also states that the figures 'do not include deaths where the underlying cause of death was natural' (*ibid.*). Such deaths from natural causes are excluded from the tables, but mentioned in footnotes. For example, the death of a person who, while engaged in a sporting activity, suffered an epileptic fit leading to an accident resulting in death, would be excluded. The OPCS data (see Table 3.1) make interesting reading.

The report breaks all the categories above down into component sports, and the category 'Other sporting and leisure activities' also shows that one death was recorded for each of the following: dancing, during children's play, model aircraft, skiing, walking, weight training. The survey also shows that there were six deaths from drowning while fishing during 1992.

The OPCS tables also record fatalities by sex and age and, as this book is concerned with young people and their involvement in Outdoor Education, it is worth looking a little more closely at this age distribution and translating the OPCS figures into the

Table 3.1 Fatal accidents (except by drowning) occurring during sporting and leisure activities, 1992

Activity	Fatal accidents
Air sports	11
Athletic sports	9
Ball games	4
Horse-riding	12
Motor sports	16
Mountaineering and climbing	7
Pedal cycling	5
Water sports	10
Other sporting and leisure activities	8
TOTAL	84

Note: There were also two spectators killed during 1992, one watching stock car racing, and one at a hunt meeting.

chart in Figure 3.1. This shows that the highest number of fatalities occurred within the 15 to 24-year-old age range and that 28 of the 84 fatalities, exactly one-third, were between the ages of 5 and 24. It may be, of course, that this merely demonstrates a greater participation in sporting activities by this age range but, given our duty of care as teachers and leaders, we must reflect on this carefully as none of us want young people for whom we are responsible to end up as a statistic.

Further research into the comparative dangers of sporting activities also illustrates the importance in differentiating between real and perceived risk. *The Sheffield Study* (1995), commissioned by the Sports' Council, sought information from a random sample of 28,000 16 to 45-year-olds on sporting activities and injuries during a set four-week period. Among other findings, the report discovered that the sport of rugby had an injury rate of 100 injuries per 1,000 'occasions of participation'. It must be acknowledged, of course, that rugby is one of the most intensively researched areas in sports medicine, with more than

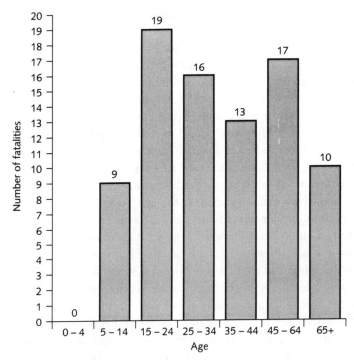

Figure 3.1 1992 fatalities

160 papers produced in the past twenty years, which have greatly improved safety standards over recent years, although the Sports' Council survey, effectively, implies that rugby players have a 1:10 chance of injury every time they take to the field. However, I would contend that parents often have a greater fear of the risks, whether real or perceived, associated with mountaineering, rock-climbing, skiing and the like, than they do of the real risks of injury associated with sports such as rugby.

This apparent contradiction is, perhaps, borne out by a report in the *Times Educational Supplement* (Wolf, 1994, p. 10) which stated that, although riding or pony trekking, as part of an activity holiday, may appear benign, 'It is a sobering thought that over the past ten years there have been nearly 200 riding fatalities' and that a study into holiday activity centres in Wales had found that 'horse riding produced one of the highest rates of injury compared with other outdoor activities'. The report goes on to state that the Riding Establishments Act 1964 required that, although centres were licensed by the local authority, escorts on rides and treks need only be 'a responsible person of the age of 16 years or over and competent to ride without supervision'. This meant that the escort need not be qualified in first aid or have any idea what to do if there was an accident. On first impressions, this does not seem to sit squarely alongside the requirements of leadership qualifications for other outdoor activities where schemes such as the Basic Expedition Training Award, Ski Leader awards and the awards of the Mountain-walking Leader Training Boards, along with many other similar outdoor leadership awards, require that holders of such qualifications possess a current first aid certificate which has to be renewed at least every three years. To be fair, the report emphasized that the British Horse Society was considerably more stringent in its requirements for including establishments in its annual *Where to Ride* guide, and has a code of conduct for pony trekking, which stables have to meet if they are to gain the society's approval. This code stipulates that groups should be of a limited size, that escorts should have a thorough knowledge of road safety, an elementary knowledge of first aid and carry a first aid kit with them at all times. The HSC *Guidance on Regulations* (1996) also states that a group leader should hold a BHS Tourism Qualification for Ride Leader.

As an aside, while considering this apparent contradiction in people's reactions to real and perceived risks, it is interesting to note that, in reporting the appointment of eight senior inspectors, from the traditional fields of mountaineering, canoeing, sailing, etc., to the new Adventure Activities Licensing Authority (AALA), the *National Association for Outdoor Education Newsletter* (1996) noted that the AALA had also appointed a part-time specialist to watch out for 'dangerous activities, i.e. really dangerous not apparently dangerous. His experience is in things like the inspection of Brands Hatch and the Nurnberger Ring for Formula One motor racing'.

This view is, to some extent, supported by looking at how insurance companies view the risks associated by various sports where rugby, horse-riding, yachting and boxing are at the high end of the scale and some activities, such as acrobatics, bob-sleighing and caving are classed as extra-hazardous for third-party liability purposes. Worthy of note, from our perspective as responsible leaders or teachers, is the fact that, through looking at the calculated insurers' risks it is apparent that so few amateur sportsmen or schoolchildren appear to be covered by any form of insurance cover. Tony O'Brien (1995), insurance specialist for the Central Council for Physical Recreation, which represents all governing bodies of sport, estimates that up to 80 per cent of schoolchildren lack even basic cover. The lesson to be learnt here, of course, is that no matter how carefully we assess and minimize risk, it is always best to be covered for any eventuality and we will be considering this, with regard to planning outdoor experiences, in Chapter 4.

Like all statistics, the figures quoted above, from both OPCS and the Sports' Council, need careful interpretation and, although this chapter is not the place for such analysis, it is important to remember that even though such statistics can calculate the mathematical odds of injury or death, they can never predict when such an unfortunate event will actually occur. However, the figures do provoke some interesting discussion with regard to the risks associated with Outdoor Education. It may be that, although very real risks undoubtedly exist within all outdoor activities, the framework in which they are undertaken provides safety mechanisms to reduce these risks to acceptable levels. This is, at present, a common theme in industrial risk assessment where employers are required to consider not only the hazard itself, but the likelihood of it actually occurring. This often puts the emphasis on to the supervisor of any potentially dangerous activity as, if the likelihood of an accident happening was assessed to very low, and then an incident does occur, something must have gone wrong in the management of the activity. This emphasis on the supervisor or leader has long been a feature of Outdoor Education where all governing bodies of sport responsible for outdoor activities have stringent leader training programmes which ensure that, in general, such activities undertaken with young people are done so by qualified and experienced leaders within a rigid framework of safety.

Recognizing and appreciating risk

Risk happens in our everyday lives, although sometimes we do not acknowledge it. Every field of human endeavour is fraught with potential dangers. Each time we plug in an electric kettle, we have a possible, mathematical, risk of electrocution. But this is not uppermost in our minds, as the chances are so small. Nevertheless it happens, and the people it happens to were not expecting it! So could it be that the notion of expectation helps us to put the concept of risk into context? When we buy a lottery ticket there is, in reality, a very high expectation of losing and we are, therefore, consciously risking our £1 coin. When rock-climbing, for example, we may, likewise, have a statistical chance of falling to our death, but we do not expect to do so, in the same way as we make a comparison of hazard against likelihood in an industrial setting as mentioned earlier. However, on a rock-face, the consequences of taking on the risk are greater; we may pay with our lives. Is our perception of risk dependent, therefore, on the scale of what we have at stake? This is a view which may be borne out by Laura Davies, the world number one women's golfer, reported in the press as losing £500,000 on gambling in recent years, who stated that it seldom bothered her if she lost, as she could afford to do so. If this is put into context against her tournament winnings of $1 million a year, we can see that, although the financial value of the gambling money at 'risk' is high, it is arguably as much in perspective as a person on income support risking £1 every week gambling on the National Lottery.

Calculating the odds

This chapter is not, of course, about gambling, although it does serve as a useful analogy as it is often the most tangible way in which the everyday person in the street comes in to conscious contact with what many consider to be the embodiment of the concept of risk. In many ways, it is a useful comparison as it demonstrates that, to a large extent, the notion of risk is all a question of scale. Most people would not risk losing their house on a bet, although they may well risk a sum of money which they consider to be disposable. But life does not always work like that. When undertaking potentially dangerous outdoor pursuits, the risk factor (i.e., one life) is constant and it may be that we perceive risk, therefore, in slightly different terms. A Royal Society report, *Risk: Analysis, Perception and Management* (1992), suggests that: 'Whereas risk once meant the probability of losses and gains . . . it now just means danger' (p. 113). This would certainly be the case in Outdoor Education where the concept of risk is associated with the safe management of danger. So what gives us, as leaders or teachers, our understanding of risk in the outdoors so vital to the reduction of risk to acceptable levels and, ideally, our attempted elimination, of it? It could be argued that we can tame risk through experience and, although this is certainly the case, it is not totally infallible, indeed, regardless of experience, human error is blamed for nineteen out of twenty road traffic accidents. In countering the argument that, as a mother with two young children, Alison Hargreaves, the mountaineer who, in May 1995, had just become the first woman to conquer Everest without oxygen, took too many risks, family friend Bill O'Connor stated that: 'Alison is very much against taking risks. Climbers like Alison make judgements based on their knowledge and skills. It is this attitude which makes her a first-class climber' (Johnstone, 1995). Barely three months after her ascent of Everest, Alison tragically died on the Himalayan mountain K2 in August 1995.

However, this attitude towards risk is no different from the sentiments of many others who pursue potentially dangerous pursuits at high levels, in that they do not, generally, have a death wish. They believe that they can take on the risk and tame it through their ability, skill and experience. This is undeniably true, but an element of risk always remains. In fact, what would be the purpose if risk was not there? Lord Hunt, the leader of the first successful Everest Expedition in 1953, has been quoted as saying that without an element of risk, mountaineering would be worthless; a safety net would defeat the *raison d'être* of mountaineering, that of conquering the elements. This view is supported by Sir Robin Knox-Johnston, the distinguished sailor who said that, in terms of adventure and risk:

> Humans have been doing this since we evolved. They went out
> with great big clubs and beat mammoths over the head, or lanced
> them, which was very risky. If something is difficult, almost
> impossible to achieve, then it is worth doing. (Quoted in Driscoll,
> 1997, p. 14)

In a feature in the *Sunday Times*, Margarette Driscoll (1997) wrote on why modern adventurers leave loving families and pit their lives against the most hostile elements and quoted Sir Chris Bonington on taking risks for the sheer fun of it:

> There is no doubt about it that the element of risk gives
> exploratory climbing extra spice. It is quite addictive. Playing the
> risk game is a powerful stimulus, therefore, if you become used to
> that stimulus, the excitement, you want to go on with it.

John Adams rationalizes this ethos with the notion of risk compensation. He suggests that 'accident losses are, by definition, a consequence of taking risks; the more risks an individual takes, the greater, on average, will be both the rewards and losses he or she incurs' (Adams, 1995, p. 15). This may also be a clue to the motivational factors influencing Alison Hargreaves whose husband, Jim Ballard, stated in the *Observer*, a week after she died, that, had she survived, she would have been 'at the beginning of her life as a celebrity. She could support the family for life. She would never have to do a climb again' (Beaumont and Douglas, 1995).

A risk ratio

Wally Keay, a past Chairman of the Mountainwalking Leader Training Board and Technical and Safety Adviser to The Duke of Edinburgh's Award, once proposed that safety could be viewed as the following formula:

safety = e × t × p × E
where: e = equipment, t = training, p = planning, E = experience and they are all in equilibrium

This is an eloquent method of conveying the concept of safety and it is worth considering whether we can apply a similar approach to the providing a solution to the notion of risk. If so, we could end up with an equation which was simply:

risk = E − P
E = everything that may go wrong
P = all the precautions we have taken against E

Although this is slightly tongue-in-cheek, it illustrates that the scope of risk is so wide as to make it impossible to legislate against every possible eventuality. Instead, however, why not approach the problem from the opposite end and consider a formula for recognizing risk. In the same way that followers of horse-racing study a horse's form to help them try to predict the outcome of a race (their risk assessment) and their subsequent betting affects the bookmakers' odds (the mathematical or statistical chances of the event happening, their likelihood), could we devise a similar mathematical process to calculate the element of risk in the outdoors? As we have seen earlier, we can interrogate all available statistics of injuries and deaths to arrive at a precise statistical equation of the incidence of accidents and injury, and this, in a way, is our 'odds'. We should, however, equally concern ourselves with the 'form' of all the various factors influencing the activity so that we take appropriate preventative measures to ensure that an incident does not occur. As racegoers consider a horse's performance in previous races, can we make allowances for past experience, skills and knowledge?

To illustrate this idea, we shall consider a hypothetical situation at the perceived edges of risk, free-fall parachuting from an aeroplane at 20,000 feet. First, we need to ascertain what, at the bottom line, is at risk. In this case, and for ease of illustration, we shall say that a life is at stake, in that this is an individual activity where the most likely result of serious misfortune (such as the parachute and reserve parachute not functioning) is death. We then have to arrive at a formula for aggregating out experience, our 'form' in horse racing terms. However, we do not have the published results of previous races to look back on, so what exactly should we take into consideration? One obvious factor would, of course, be previous experience. In very simple terms, let us assume that each full year of experience (encompassing skills, confidence and knowledge acquired along the way) is worth a factor of ten. We can then produce a simple ratio. For a novice with less than one year's experience the sum would be 1 (life) to 10 (experience) or a ratio of 1:10. For an experienced sport parachutist with ten years' experience the sum would be 1 (life) to 100 (experience) or a ratio of 1:100. In other words, making an unplanned, instructorless, unassisted, free-fall jump from an aeroplane would give odds of 1 in 10 of failing for a novice and odds of 1 in 100 of failing for an experienced jumper. It may be that a 1:10 chance of death may be realistic for those unfortunate enough to have to bail out unexpectedly (and without any prior knowledge or training) from an aircraft.

A 1 in 10 chance of failure, even derived from such a simplistic equation as this, is obviously unacceptable, so how do we improve the odds for novices beginning an activity or pursuit; if we did not, how would anyone progress? The next step could be to add in another factor for supervision by a trainer where we could add the trainer's experience points to the novice's points to form a more acceptable risk factor. If, in the case above, the novice were to undertake a tandem jump with the experienced jumper we would have a chance of failure of 1 (life) to 10 (novice's points) + 100 (trainer's experience points) making a ratio of 1:110.

The final part of this simple equation would be to allocate points for instructor, leader or supervisor qualifications held by the experienced person. If, for example, the activity in question had three levels of instructor certification (leader, instructor, trainer) we could allocate 50 points to each level, i.e., leader = 50, instructor = 100, trainer = 150. If, to continue our example above, a novice was to undertake a tandem jump with a qualified parachute trainer with ten years' experience, the equation would be: 1 (life) to 100 (trainer's experience) + 150 (trainer's qualification) + 10 (novice's points) = 1:260. A ratio of 1:260, implying a 1:260 chance of serious mishap, may be considered a more acceptable level of risk.

Of course, the above is only a hypothetical situation, but the suggestion of analysing risk in this way is not to provide an exact numerical answer (as the number, itself, is meaningless and even analysing a horse's previous form and considering the betting odds does not guarantee a winner every time), but to develop a structure which forces leaders to think about the potential risk of situations they encounter. It is the process of considering risk which is important. To continue the horse-racing analogy used earlier, in the same way that racegoers may favour higher odds, we can also use these ratios, our 'odds', to provide a clue, or a prompt. If the odds seem too low, we should be encouraged to think again about the activity. To put this hypothetical ratio into some form of actual context, Dr Michael Turner (1994), chief medical adviser to the British Ski Team, has calculated that the chances of being injured in a day's skiing are around one in 100, while the chances of being killed are less than one in 8 million. The problem, as we have already seen, is that we can calculate the statistical chances of injury, but we cannot predict when an accident will happen. Our job is to do our best to ensure that accidents do not happen.

Once we, as leaders, have acknowledged that a risk exists, and identified it as such, we are well on the way to being able to minimize the risk (or to take appropriate action, by changing our plans, to avoid it altogether). The management of risk should be an ongoing process, a theme to which we return at each and every decision we make which involves the actions, and ultimately the safety, of others. This, in turn, should require educational managers in schools or the youth service and officials of voluntary youth organizations, to consider the qualifications and experience of staff involved in Outdoor Education. The HSE *Guidance on Regulations* recommends that

> higher levels of experience or qualifications might be required if the activity involves: novice participants in a high hazard location; conducting the activity at night or in the absence of other on-site instructors with greater experience. There may be cases where lower levels of competence would be sufficient and acceptable . . . where an activity is at a level not catered for by a nationally available qualification or where a well controlled limited site or route is used frequently. (HSE, 1996, p. 5)

Much advice on the required qualifications for leaders and instructors is given in the HSC guidance, and in other publications such as the *National Guidelines* from the UKMTB (1995).

A tool rather than a theory

So far, in the examples used above, we have assumed that the risk factor is 1, in that it refers to the fact that there is one life at risk. This is, of course, oversimplistic as our one and only life is what is always at risk, even if merely plugging in an electric kettle! It also does not allow for any refinement of calculating the risk factor. Every time we ventured into the outdoors, the stake would be the same. Although this is, of course, factually correct, it is not realistic, because it does not, as it stands, allow for the possibility of an outcome less than death such as the possibility of minor injury or the intervention of external assistance. Let us, then, look at ways of refining our equation to produce a tool or methodology to assist us with judging risks which allows practical application in the field.

Risk analysis or risk assessment

Within Health and Safety at Work regulations, European Community directives on safety, which came into effect in January 1993, made the assessment of risks a legal requirement. Employers whose workers come into contact with hazardous chemicals, equipment, processes or other potential dangers are required to undertake an assessment of the likely risk of injury as part of their company's safety management programmes. Risk assessment is generally accepted to be concerned with the probability of an accident occurring and the level of damage/injury it would cause. Such practices often use a generic risk assessment matrix, and it is an adaptation of this which can help us to refine our ratio. Such a matrix, shown in Figure 3.2, has been refined to focus on an outdoor situation, in this case a foot expedition, or a journey in wild, mountainous, country. Similar charts could be produced for any other outdoor activity using different outcomes on the 'severity' axis.

The two criteria to be considered in making such a risk assessment are the likelihood of an accident occurring – the probability – and the seriousness of any resulting injury – the severity. The probability axis has been divided into four: unlikely, possibly, probably and certainty. A fifth category or division, 'none', which could have been included at the bottom of the probability scale implying that there would definitely be no likelihood of even very minor injury, has been avoided as we can never make such an assumption; after all, people can fracture ribs from sneezing in bed! However, a 'certainty' scale must be included, as any really foolhardy action, such as

		SEVERITY			
		MINOR FIRST AID (SELF-HELP)	OUTSIDE ASSISTANCE (LEADER)	SELF-EVACUATION (GROUP)	EVACUATION (MOUNTAIN RESCUE)	SERIOUS INJURY OR DEATH
PROBABILITY	CERTAINTY					
	PROBABLY					
	POSSIBLY					
	UNLIKELY					

Figure 3.2 Risk assessment matrix

abseiling off a 50-metre cliff without tying on to a rope, would certainly lead to serious injury, and the minute mathematical possibility which exists for no injury being sustained can be discounted if we are endeavouring to produce a methodology to promote a climate for maximum safety the maximum of time (indeed, the press reported an incident in September 1995 when a 14-year-old boy fell 120 feet from a viaduct in North Yorkshire without breaking a bone, but incidents such as this are freak occurrences).

The matrix is read, in the same way as journey distance planners which are often found in road atlases, along the top and up the side and the appropriate box, within the table, ticked. The aim is to consider the activity and assess the most probable outcome, in terms of severity, if something were to go wrong. For example, if a group of young people undertake an unaccompanied morning's stroll along waymarked footpaths in normal, or open, countryside the danger – the group becoming temporarily lost – is unlikely to result in minor first aid (not even blisters) so this would fall outside the shaded area and be considered an acceptable risk. However, were their route, at one point, to include crossing a busy dual carriageway, where there was no bridge or underpass, the danger – one or more of the group being knocked down by a car – would, almost certainly, result in their serious injury or death. This outcome would fall into the shaded area and the road crossing would, therefore, be viewed as an unacceptable risk and an alternative route would have to be found, or the risk greatly reduced by positioning staff to conduct the young people safely across the road at a marked crossing point.

The matrix, as it stands, only really defines risks into two categories, acceptable and unacceptable. To be more meaningful, and to begin to enable us to look more closely at the precise nature of the risk involved, a points scoring system can be added into the matrix, as in the refined risk assessment matrix in Figure 3.3. The numbers we have put in the matrix are purely arbitrary, ranging as they do from 1 to 20. We could have used figures from 10 to 200. It is not the numbers themselves which are important, but the process which the matrix takes us through. We consider the activity we are involved in and assess the likelihood, or probability, of a range of potential negative outcomes, the severity, and use the matrix to assess whether this activity errs towards acceptable or unacceptable levels of risk.

In this refined matrix, we have begun to 'load' the assessment of potential risk on a points score between 1 to 20. We can then

		SEVERITY				
		MINOR FIRST AID (SELF-HELP)	OUTSIDE ASSISTANCE (LEADER)	SELF-EVACUATION (GROUP)	EVACUATION (MOUNTAIN RESCUE)	SERIOUS INJURY OR DEATH
PROBABILITY	CERTAINTY	4	8	12	16	20
	PROBABLY	3	6	9	12	15
	POSSIBLY	2	4	6	8	10
	UNLIKELY	1	2	3	4	5

Figure 3.3 Refined risk assessment matrix

use this to analyse the activity to be undertaken and the appropriateness of exposing the young people concerned to risk. We may decide, for example, that, in dealing with a group of primary-aged schoolchildren, a maximum risk factor of 2 would be appropriate. We may feel that if the children involved developed blisters and, thus, fell into the 'certainty – minor first aid' category, which has a score of 3, this would be unacceptable at this stage of the child's development as they do not have the necessary first aid skills to administer dressings to themselves or their friends, and the discomfort caused by walking with blisters may deter them from pursuing the activity in future. Likewise, we may feel that the children concerned lack the maturity to evacuate themselves, as a group, from any predicament in which they may find themselves, being a risk under the 'unlikely – self-evacuation' category which also scores a 3. In this model, we would acknowledge that the possibility of minor first aid existed (true in a great many things which primary-aged children undertake) and that there also existed the remote chance of the children requiring the intervention of the leader; both of which we may consider to be acceptable levels of risk as they score 2 points. To use a practical example to illustrate this more clearly, we may consider that the children undertaking an introductory navigational game in a fenced and secured field would fall into this category of risk and would be an appropriate risk for leaders or teachers to take.

Risk awareness

As stated above, the suggestion of looking at risk as a ratio, or in terms of a matrix, is not intended to provide finite numerical answers. We cannot, for example, categorically state that a ratio of 1:260 or a risk assessment factor of 2 will mean that some tragic misfortune will not affect the activity concerned. Much in the same way as bookmakers odds are not an exact indication of which horse will win a race, any number score achieved by the two means outlined above will not necessarily ensure a totally risk free experience. For that reason, the term 'risk awareness' fulfils our requirements better than the industrially used terms of risk assessment or risk analysis. We, as leaders in the outdoors, can never possibly hope to analyse or assess every possible permutation of risk every time we venture out with groups of young people. The scope is too large. The identification of risk, and an awareness and appreciation of it, cannot, in the context of Outdoor Education, be simplified into a list of specific situations to avoid, perhaps in the way that we teach children safety in the kitchen. In this respect, we have to be clear that we are attempting to assess and appreciate risk as a complex concept, rather than identifying specific dangers, and in so doing, are allowing our awareness of risk to influence our planning and preparation.

There are, in all risk situations, factors outside our control. In the outdoors the effects of external influences, such as the weather, the environment and the compliance (or behaviour) of the group can alter at a moments notice and have a far-reaching effect on the outcome of our activity. Such factors must be taken into account, as a possibility, in every situation to provide a theoretical safety net for the activities we wish to undertake. Foot expeditions are encouraged to plan an alternative route for bad weather as a sensible safety precaution even though there is the anticipation of the weather being suitable for the completion of the intended route. This should become good practice in all we do; the planning of alternatives to be used in the event of our risk awareness procedures indicating that the planned activity cannot precede. We would, of course, be totally wrong to adopt the opposite stance and attempt to merely appreciate risk in terms of operating in an ideal world, when the weather is permanently good, the environment kind and the group immaculately well behaved.

It may be, then, that the matrix outlined in Figure 3.3, requires modification in the field to suit the specific and individual circumstances in which leaders finds themselves. With a badly behaved or disruptive group of primary pupils, or in

torrential rain, the practical example quoted above, of an introductory navigational game in an enclosed and secure field, may
have a higher associated risk of mishap than if undertaken with
charming pupils on an idyllic afternoon. How, then, can we
build such inconsistencies into our calculations? A simple answer
would be to apply a 'factor-plan' loading the scores in accord-
ance with the unpredictability of the external influence. For
example, we could multiply the numbers in each box in the
matrix (the matrix score) by a factor of two for bad weather, we
could multiply them by three for unpredictable environment
and multiply them by four for lack of compliance on behalf of
the group. This will have quite dramatic effects on our overall
matrix score, which, although in itself, as we have seen, is a
meaningless number, serves as our indicator of potential risk.

This factor-plan of multiplying the matrix score in each of the
original boxes to allow for other influencing factors has been
applied to Figure 3.4 and we can see, for example, that our score
for an activity certainly requiring minor first aid grows from a
reasonable 4 to an unacceptable 16 if we are working with an
unruly or non-compliant group. This is, realistically, what we
would expect, as a group of primary children charging around
a field are very likely to suffer minor cuts, scrapes and bruises.
The final chart shows each of the boxes of the original matrix
divided into quarters. The bottom left-hand quarter represents
activities taking place in ideal situations. The top left-hand
quarter represents activities taking place in inclement weather.
The top right-hand quarter represents activities taking place in a
hostile environment or terrain, while the bottom right-hand
quarter represents activities taking place with an unruly or non-
compliant group, as illustrated diagrammatically in Figure 3.4a.

A small problem here is that we are beginning to have an
extremely complicated looking matrix which resembles loga-
rithm tables rather than a handy ready-reckoner providing
an awareness of risk. The major failing, however, is that the
numbers do not reflect the permutations possible when a situation occurs in which all three external influences apply, in that a

		SEVERITY				
		MINOR FIRST AID (SELF-HELP)	OUTSIDE ASSISTANCE (LEADER)	SELF-EVACUATION (GROUP)	EVACUATION (MOUNTAIN RESCUE)	SERIOUS INJURY OR DEATH
PROBABILITY	CERTAINTY	8 ¦ 12	16 ¦ 24	24 ¦ 36	32 ¦ 48	40 ¦ 60
		4 ¦ 16	8 ¦ 32	12 ¦ 48	16 ¦ 64	20 ¦ 80
	PROBABLY	6 ¦ 9	12 ¦ 18	18 ¦ 27	24 ¦ 36	30 ¦ 45
		3 ¦ 12	6 ¦ 24	9 ¦ 36	12 ¦ 48	15 ¦ 60
	POSSIBLY	4 ¦ 6	8 ¦ 12	12 ¦ 18	16 ¦ 24	20 ¦ 30
		2 ¦ 8	4 ¦ 16	6 ¦ 24	8 ¦ 32	10 ¦ 40
	UNLIKELY	2 ¦ 3	4 ¦ 6	6 ¦ 9	8 ¦ 12	10 ¦ 15
		1 ¦ 4	2 ¦ 8	3 ¦ 12	4 ¦ 16	5 ¦ 20

Figure 3.4   Risk awareness matrix

Top Left   Top Right

WEATHER CONDITIONS	ENVIRONMENT AND TERRAIN
IDEAL SITUATION	COMPLIANCE OF GROUP

Bottom Left   Bottom Right

Figure 3.4a   Risk awareness matrix box

leader has a non-compliant group, in an unpredictable environment and in bad weather. We must, therefore, have the flexibility to multiply all these factors to have a cumulative effect. This can be done by using the original refined risk assessment matrix from Figure 3.3 and adding the chart in Figure 3.4b.

The simple addition to our original risk awareness matrix would, therefore, be to take the matrix score (M, the number in the box which has been selected to identify the risk awareness factor) and multiply it by the number shown in Figure 3.4b, within the shaded boxes, for whichever external influence,

A	weather conditions	good	1	inclement	2
B	environment/terrain	benign	1	hostile	3
C	group behaviour	compliant	1	disruptive	4

Figure 3.4b Risk awareness cumulative effect

weather, environment or group behaviour applies. Written as an equation, this would appear as: M × A × B × C = risk awareness score.

To work through a practical example. Take a score on the matrix, for example 6, where self-evacuation was a possibility. Assuming that the only negative external influence was bad weather, the sum would be 6 × 2 × 1 × 1 = 12. This puts the activity (with a total risk awareness score of 12) in the same category as 'certainly – self-evacuation' and 'probably – evacuation by a mountain rescue team' and we would have to look again at our plans to design out such risks and choose a more sensible option. Things would get even worse if we had a combination of bad weather, hostile terrain and a disruptive group, when the sum would be 6 × 2 × 3 × 4 = 144, a much higher, and totally unacceptable, score.

The final Risk Awareness Matrix is, therefore, as shown in Figure 3.5.

Efficacy or effectiveness?

Now that we have developed a system for making us aware of the nature and potential for risk we have to consider putting it into practice. This risk awareness approach must be incorporated within our general planning for outdoor experiences which will be considered in Chapter 4. Although safety is an absolute priority, we must be equally concerned with the content of our programmes. Safety, quality and delivery must all be in balance. Ski instructors and trainers talk of 'selling' the sport, SEL being an acronym for safety, enjoyment and learning, and this is a

		SEVERITY				
		MINOR FIRST AID (SELF-HELP)	OUTSIDE ASSISTANCE (LEADER)	SELF-EVACUATION (GROUP)	EVACUATION (MOUNTAIN RESCUE)	SERIOUS INJURY OR DEATH
PROBABILITY	CERTAINTY	4	8	12	16	20
	PROBABLY	3	6	9	12	15
	POSSIBLY	2	4	6	8	10
	UNLIKELY	1	2	3	4	5

The number in the box selected is termed matrix score (M)

A	weather conditions	good	1	inclement	2
B	environment/terrain	benign	1	hostile	3
C	group behaviour	compliant	1	disruptive	4

$M \times A \times B \times C$ = risk awareness factor

Figure 3.5 Final risk awareness matrix

valid approach to all we do. Was it not Plato in *The Republic* who said: 'Do not use compulsion, but let your children's lessons take the form of play. You will learn more about their natural abilities that way'? If the activity is safe and enjoyable, learning will often result automatically; it is our job to ensure that the participants have recognized that it has occurred. We must aim to provide a situation where we have harmony between safety and enjoyment. We do not want our analysis of risk to focus on safety at the expense of quality as it is, obviously, possible to enhance both. Of course, the ultimate, and ridiculous, extreme approach to safety through risk assessment is not to take part in any activity which is identified, in the remotest sense, as a risk. Although such a policy would be totally effective, it would not be efficacious as it would not produce the desired effect of promoting the personal and social development of our young people. We must, therefore, accept that we have to confront the ethical dilemma of balancing the educational benefits of the activity against the exposure to risk. Such a situation brings to mind an entertaining letter from a Mr Arnold Catterall, in *The Times* (13 January 1997), which referred to a recent survey of motor insurance which had identified that one insurance company's perfect low risk customer was a Fiat driver, living in Suffolk and driving mainly on motorways. The letter pointed out that there are no motorways in Suffolk!

Quantifying the risk

The final part of putting our risk awareness procedures into practice is to ensure that we are vigilant and consistent in our approach. As leaders, we must never miss an opportunity of analysing the potential risk and considering all possibilities for remedial action. This is not in an attempt to wrap our charges in cotton wool so that nothing can harm them, but to take practical steps to minimize the dangers. The same enjoyment and fun can be had from riding a bicycle whether or not you are wearing a helmet, gloves and protective clothing; it is only when you fall off that you notice the difference!

If we are going to attempt to provide a mechanism for producing an awareness of risks it would be beneficial if we were able to make any assessment in a way that would not only be quick and effective but would provide a permanent record of the fact that we took the care to analyse the potential dangers to which we were exposing our young people. Keeping records, as we shall see in Chapter 4, is part and parcel of good group management as it fulfils two vital functions. First, it provides us with a basis for making consistent future assessments in that the same process is used for all the varied outdoor activities with which we are involved. Second, it provides us with documentary evidence, or proof should it be required in this increasingly litigious world, that we made such assessments before exposing young people to potential hazard.

This is an ideology to which Tom Price, a past-President of the British Mountaineering Council and of the National Association for Outdoor Education, referred in an address to The Duke of Edinburgh's Award National Expedition Conference at Mark Mason's Hall, St James, in 1984, when he stated:

> There is an element of risk in everything man undertakes, indeed, even in life itself. The way to reduce this risk is not through lists of rules, equipment and clothing but through the development of judgement, vigilance, common sense, self-knowledge and prudence.

It is crucial, as we shall see later in Chapter 6 on problem-solving, that a logical and safe approach to potentially hazardous activities, and the development of this judgemental and prudent attitude, is encouraged in our young people as well as being adopted by us as leaders. *National Guidelines*, published by the UK Mountain Training Board, states that

> from the records of incidents and accidents it seems evident that many incidents could and should have been avoided. Many accidents occur as a direct result of poor planning and management and an inadequate assessment of the risks involved. One of the primary reasons for incidents is the failure to assess objectively the needs of the individual participants in relation to the activity, choice of venue and prevailing conditions. (UKMTB, 1995, p. 14)

So what practical measures can we take to ensure that we do not fall foul of this bad management of the risks involved?

Possibly the largest potential pitfall is to consider the activity rather than the individual. The activity and those undertaking it must always be considered together. To make a simple example, an introductory session on an indoor climbing wall, with a group under instruction, has two subsets of factors to be considered: the constants and the variables. The constants, things such as the wall itself, the lighting and heating (the environment) and the available equipment will always remain largely the same. They will stay constant. The variables will, obviously, vary. The number of people in the group under instruction, their ages, previous experience, special physical or emotional needs will all vary from group to group, and even from session to session with the same group. The instructor, even if the same person always instructs the session (and possibly then becomes a constant), may vary from session to session depending upon their moods, emotions and motivation, their increasing experience and the developing rapport with the group and the growing abilities of individuals within it.

This 'person-centred' philosophy is nicely summarized by Bob Barton (1994, p. 7), from Outward Bound, who says that his organization 'does not just personally develop high-flying company executives; school parties, physically and mentally handicapped people and the over-59s are put through their paces' and that central to the Outward Bound mission is 'the ideal of serving others and valuing people. Disregard for safety is out of keeping with such teaching'. So how is this approach to safety and the management of risk accomplished in practice and implemented as a natural part of our planning process?

It is the process of risk evaluation which is important

As we have already seen, it is the recognition of the existence of risk or danger in outdoor activities, and the subsequent modification of our plans to minimize this risk, which is vital. No matter what mathematical formulae we conjure up with regard to the statistical possibility of incidents occurring, we still need to demonstrate that this has not misled us into complacency. As leaders, it is the thought processes involved in the evaluation, assessment or appreciation of risk which, having made us aware of the risks involved, allow us to plan our activities to be appropriate to the client group with which we are working. Although it is the result of our risk awareness procedures (in that they will, hopefully, lead to total safety as a prime objective), the process of the exercise of risk analysis is equally as important. In which case, therefore, we need to develop a system of risk awareness which is convenient to use and consistent in its results. A simple form such as that in Figure 3.6 could provide us with a mechanism which takes us through the process of risk awareness and, in considering both extremes of risk, the 'worst case' risk as well as the 'most likely' risk, lets us make any necessary modifications to our plans rationally and sensibly, being neither to complacent about severe risks or overcautious about the minor eventualities which are bound to occur.

Such a form can me modified to suit individual needs and, as stated earlier, has the benefit of providing documentary evidence that all risks associated with the activity were considered. The form can be used in a variety of ways. The leader, individually, could work through the exercise as part of their overall planning for the activity, or they may choose to work through the form as a group with all the other staff involved on the trip. A variation on this would be for each member of the staff team to complete a form as an individual and then use all the forms as the basis of a group discussion analysing all the variables until an overall consensus of opinion was reached. It may be that, as part of their organization's overall monitoring of safety practices, the leader responsible for the activity works through the form with their line-manager justifying, in discussion, the entries. It would also be possible, as part of the process of empowering young people into accepting responsibility, that the participants themselves could complete a form, as a team, discussing the worst case and most likely risks.

Whatever the methodology used in completing the form, it is important that the process is undertaken professionally. Current good practice promotes the concept of risk awareness in all forms of Outdoor Education and the legislative standard to which we should aspire, or aim to exceed, is clear on this point. The HSE *Guidance on Regulations* states:

ACTIVITY	
Dates of activity	
Environment	
Age of participants	
Experience of participants	
'Worst case' risk	
Outcome	
Preventative measures	
Most likely risk	
Outcome	
Preventative measures	
Supervision required	
Modifications required to planned activity	

Modifications required to equipment	
Activity safe to proceed?	
Name of person making risk assessment	
Position	
Relevant qualifications	

Figure 3.6 Risk awareness form

> The primary duty to ensure the safety of young people using facilities for adventure activities rests with the provider of those facilities. The provider must therefore have a systematic approach to recognising risks and making sure something is done to control them – a safety management system. (HSE, 1996, p. 2)

Whether or not we use the form illustrated here, an auditable system should be in place and be part of our standard operating practices. An example of a completed form is given in Figure 3.7.

Additionally, the use of forms such as the above example help us in several important ways. It shows that we have identified the hazards created by the activity; that we have decided who might be harmed, and how; that we have evaluated the risk and decided whether existing precautions are adequate or more should be done; and, most importantly, that we have recorded our findings. If this process is carried out each time we work with a group in the outdoors, it also demonstrates that we review the assessment periodically and revise it if necessary. All of the above are requirements of the adventurous activities licensing scheme. Indeed, the HSE *Guidance on Regulations* states:

> The scope of the risk assessment should be sufficient to identify the significant (non-trivial) risks arising from the activity. It should be

81

Activity	Unaccompanied day walk.
Dates of activity	Mid July.
Environment	Hills, routed well away from crags or any other possible area for falls.
Age of participants	Sixth formers.
Experience of participants	Well trained. Activity is part of Sports Studies A level. This is their third day walk.
'Worst case' risk	Extreme wet and cold leading to hypothermia.
Outcome	If hypothermia sufficiently severe, possibly death.
Preventative measures	Well equipped (tent, sleeping bags, food). Well trained. Weather forecast obtained.
Most likely risk	Blisters.
Outcome	Discomfort, no lasting damage.
Preventative measures	Group carrying blister treatments in first aid kits and trained in their use. Boots well worn-in. Knowledge of possible outcomes.
Supervision required	Leaders in area of walk, no more than two kilometres away at any one time. A manned base checkpoint, with telephone access, at start or end of walk.
Modifications required to planned activity	Thorough check of route. Up-to-date weather forecast.

Modifications required to equipment	Thorough equipment check.
Activity safe to proceed?	Yes.
Name of person making risk assessment	Eleanor Hanson.
Position	Leader in charge.
Relevant qualifications	MLTB (Summer) Award. First Aid Certificate.

Figure 3.7 Completed risk awareness form

> suitable to enable the provider to identify and prioritise the measures that need to be taken to ensure, so far as is reasonably practicable, the safety of participants or others who may be affected by the activity. (HSE, 1996, p. 3)

Whether or not our work falls within scope of the scheme, the process provides evidence that we are meeting the requirements of current best practice.

Self-audit

We can also use our records of past forms to periodically undertake two other vital functions. First, we can use the process of completing the forms to undertake a self-audit; to look at our responses to the questions posed by the form and check how well prepared we are to deal with both the 'worst case risk' and the 'most likely risk'. It is important for us as leaders to have thought through and prepared a plan to be put into operation if, by some slim chance, the worst case risk actually occurred. This may involve us in additional work before the venture, but that will be more than compensated by the efficiency of our actions should something go wrong. Such additional precautions need not necessarily be elaborate. The example cited in Figure 3.7 above may prompt us to carry an extra survival bag and a flask of hot drink with us in our leader's sack, or we may feel that, as the area in which we are to be walking is so far removed from habitation, we should have an additional member of staff, in the minibus, 'shadowing' the route along the nearest road, waiting at certain prearranged locations at certain times, so that they will be in easy reach should it be necessary to bring the party off the hill. Likewise, we should also look at how well we are prepared to cope with the most likely risk. In the case of the example quoted above, we know that our group of sixth formers may well get blisters, so we must ask how well equipped they, and indeed we, are to deal with them.

Safety audit

Secondly, the completed forms and records of any remedial action taken during our outdoor experiences over the course of a year, provide us with raw data with which to undertake an annual safety audit; to evaluate and review our safety procedures and mechanisms. It may even be that we want someone external to our own organization, or at least not involved in the operation and delivery of the actual activities, to undertake this task as an outsider's eye can often spot things which, being so closely tied up to all the other aspects of our programmes, we miss. Care must be taken, however, to ensure that there is a realistic appreciation of procedures and that any potential for risk is not quashed by any 'overkill' of regulations, rules or conditions. We saw earlier in this chapter that there is a fundamental risk in everything we do, even using an electric kettle. However, manufacturers of such appliances are not legally required (yet) to have eye-catching notices on kettles stating 'This appliance is potentially dangerous. Before use ensure that you are wearing a face mask, full protective clothing, rubber shoes and that you turn on the electricity supply with a insulated stick'. This, of course, is ridiculous, but it does appear in some quarters to be an approach which is growing in use in an attempt to protect manufacturers from litigation. *Outdoor Education*

– *Safety and Good Practice* states:

> In a unique way Outdoor Education has a dynamic contribution to
> make to the health and development of individuals. Safety in
> Outdoor Education is of paramount importance. Society would be
> the poorer if restrictive regulations were to stifle the adventurous
> and enquiring spirit. (*Outdoor Education – Safety and Good
> Practice*, 1988, p. 37)

A rule of thumb for leaders

To ensure that all the theory of risk awareness and evaluation is
put into practice, we could, of course, take our final risk awareness matrix from Figure 3.5 and reproduce it onto a credit-card
sized piece of plastic to carry around with us all the time to be
able to refer to it when making decisions. However, much of our
risk assessment and awareness should have taken place at the
planning stage, considered in Chapter 4, when we can consider
all eventualities and alternatives in a calm frame of mind rather
than making pressured assessments in the field. In this situation,
we need a rule of thumb, the simpler the better. One method, to
paraphrase the outdoor educator and mountaineer John Jackson,
is to ask yourself, as a leader: 'Am I; in the right place; at the
right time; with the right people; with the right equipment?' As
Chris Loynes says in the editorial to an edition of *Adventure
Education and Outdoor Leadership*:

> In the last analysis it is not rules that will make people safer, it is
> the sound judgement of the leader in the field constantly assessing
> a dynamic range of factors that makes the difference. There is no
> substitute for experience. (Loynes, 1996, p. 15)

In the final analysis, we should be considering all our actions
with risk awareness at the back of our minds. This can be seen
as an attitude, or approach, to being a leader in the outdoors
where, on our credit-card sized *aide-mémoire*, armed with the
thought processes which the rest of this chapter has taken us
through, we continually ask ourselves the following questions:

85

- Have I exercised sound judgement at all times?
- Have I taken all reasonable safety precautions?
- Have I acted responsibly?

And, just for good measure, on the back of the card we could ask ourselves the catch-all 'sixty-four thousand dollar' question: ARE YOU SURE?

4 We want information, information, information: The importance of planning and preparation in Outdoor Education

> Politics is perhaps the only profession for which
> no preparation is thought necessary.
> Robert Louis Stevenson, *Familiar Studies*
> *of Men and Books* (1882)

Introduction

Thomas Alva Edison (1847–1931) once said: 'Genius is one per cent inspiration and ninety-nine per cent perspiration' (*Life* magazine, 1932). This can be paraphrased to state that, from an educational viewpoint, leadership in the outdoors is 1 per cent perspiration and 99 per cent organization. We have already seen, in Chapter 3, that a prime consideration of using the outdoors as a vehicle for the personal and social development of young people is in enhancing adventure and learning while minimizing risk, and it is largely through detailed planning and thorough preparation – in short, being organized – that this is accomplished. For this reason, every minute aspect of the venture or outdoor experience must be planned in detail and nothing left to chance. This is a task so potentially large that it is impossible to ad lib and a framework, or model, for planning the experience or venture must be devised. With sufficient prior preparation and thought, added to our growing experience, we can reduce a great amount of the stress involved in remembering all the little details by, quite literally, ticking the boxes. Preparing for any outdoor experience should be a logical process with a number of key stages and half the battle will have been won if we can adopt a logistical, or project management, approach to our planning.

The distinct stages of planning

Before we consider what we plan, we should consider how we plan. I have always maintained that, no matter what area we work in, it requires a great deal of preparation and hard work to give the appearance of being 'laid back'; it takes an organized approach to truly work well with flexible work patterns. Leaving tasks until later is not the same thing at all. This is especially true in any form of long-term project where, if one has thought through every possible detail in advance, and put the correct operational procedures into place, one can have the luxury of enjoying the actual event. If, however, everything has been left to the last minute, the event will be lost in a haze of crisis management. There is no such thing as retrospective planning.

In this respect, an outdoor experience is no different from any other event, in that it has three, self-evident, evolutionary divisions: before, during and after. All are equally important, in terms of the successful outcome of the venture, and all must be planned for, although it will be likely that the 'before' stage will take up a greater proportion of time and effort. March and Wattchow (1991), writing on the importance of the expedition in adventure education, expand the before, during and after into four distinct phases which they feel are critical to the total expedition experience and which they name:

- The Conceptualization/Dream Phase
- The Preparation Phase
- The Action/Reality Phase
- The Reporting/Reflective/Processing Phase

This is a variation on a theme which is often used, diagrammatically, to show the ongoing process of planning, doing and reviewing, applicable to any form of experience, such as in the much used Kolb cycle which also uses four stages or phases (Figure 4.1).

The Kolb cycle implies, by its circular nature, that it is possible to enter the cycle at any point. Although this may be true, in that the start point could be 'having an adventure', it would imply that, if this so, the experience had not been fully planned. This may often be the case with personal events when an opportunity, too good to miss, simply presents itself, but it is not education-ally viable if we are framing Outdoor Education in the context of the personal and social development of young people; we would be failing in our duties as responsible leaders if an adventure, especially if it involved any element of risk, was not planned. We must, therefore, accept that, in an educational sense, there can be only two possible entry points into the cycle: either the planning of a future experience, or the reviewing of a past experience laying the foundation for a possible future project. This previous experience need not necessarily be our own, as we may, of course, be motivated to copy the exploits of others and plan our own adventures from their inspiration.

If we are planning future expeditions from our own past experience, the cycle of planning, doing and reviewing becomes transformed into a spiral, or a series of enlarging concentric circles. This cyclical structure has been in common use for many years and outdoor centres, such as Brathay Hall in Cumbria, have long used similar models in their development training

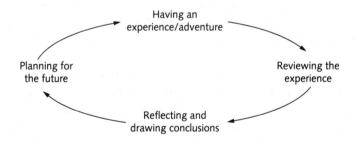

Figure 4.1 The Kolb cycle

work. Wally Keay (1996) in *Expedition Guide* (p. 408) expresses this cycle succinctly by illustrating it as a continuous process of:

PLAN, DO, REVIEW,
PLAN AGAIN, DO AGAIN, REVIEW,
PLAN AGAIN, DO AGAIN, REVIEW,
etc.

It is certainly the case that the process of planning, doing and reviewing is, indeed, cyclical in nature, in that it is an ongoing, rolling process in which we gain experience from each venture, which is carried forward to assist in the planning and execution of subsequent ventures. However, I believe that, in reality, the planning for our ventures tends to be linear. This is because, in organizational terms, it is important for each venture to be seen as a separate entity, with its own individual 'history' and, as such, planned and undertaken from start to finish. It may be, of course, that the end of one venture leads on, through our increased experience and enthusiasm, to the start of the next, thus constituting a cycle, but this is then a cycle of learning, not of planning. It is, naturally, only to be expected that our personal experience as planners will grow, but we should not allow any element of complacency to creep in nor be tempted to use experience gained from previous ventures as a short-cut in planning the next. There should be no room for the notion that we have undertaken the activity, with different groups of participants, so often in the past that we do not need to diligently work through all the stages of planning. Circumstances change and the experience is fresh to each new group of young people with whom we work. We must use our experience, not abuse it.

We are, in the context of this chapter, considering the promotion of best practice in planning any form of Outdoor Education experience and, to this end, it is vital that our planning process produces an auditable trail of evidence proving that we have given each stage of every venture the care and attention to detail which it deserves. There must, therefore, be

MARCH and WATTCHOW	THE KOLB CYCLE
Conceptualization/Dream Phase	
Preparation Phase	Planning for the future
Action/Reality Phase	Having an experience/adventure
Reporting/Reflective Processing Phase	Reviewing the experience
	Drawing conclusions from the experience

Figure 4.2 March and Wattchow phases in comparison with the Kolb cycle

a clear distinction between every venture with each being its own self-contained package with a clearly defined beginning and an equally clear end. This can be illustrated by rearranging the Kolb cycle into a linear process and comparing it against March and Wattchow's four phases as in Figure 4.2.

We can see, from Figure 4.2, that the basic concept of before,

MARCH and WATTCHOW	THE KOLB CYCLE	
Conceptualization/Dream Phase		**CONCEPT**
Preparation Phase	Planning for the future	**PLANNING**
Action/Reality Phase	Having an experience/adventure	**ACTION**
Reporting/Reflective Processing Phase	Reviewing the experience	**REFLECTION**
	Drawing conclusions from the experience	**REVIEW**

Figure 4.3 The phases/stages of a venture

during and after is expanded by both the March and Wattchow model and the Kolb cycle into four stages. The first gives more emphasis to the initiation of a venture, while the second focuses more heavily on the post-venture activities. This, to me, implies that there are, in fact, five divisions to any experience which I have identified within the shaded boxes in Figure 4.3. Put simply, we start with an idea, we plan, we do, we reflect and then we review. Concept and planning are the 'before', action is the 'during' and the reflection and review are the 'after'.

If the venture, or activity, has five key stages, we must give them all equal status and importance although there may, of course, be differentials in terms of time. Each stage will require considerable thought, preparation and planning; they will not happen automatically. We will see later, in Chapter 7, how important it is to plan for the stages following the experience, although it should already be considered best practice for the same care and attention to be given to all phases of the venture. All this planning should add up to one thing; the quality of the TOTAL experience.

These five stages of planning, illustrated in Figure 4.4, do not

CONCEPT
The initial idea, the inspiration, the vision. Either our own, or replicating the exploits of others.
PLANNING
Turning the concept into firm plans. Anticipating and preparing for every eventuality.
ACTION
Turning the plans into reality. Undertaking the venture, the doing, being there.
REFLECTION
Looking back at the experience. The learning, the memories, the emotions, the photographs.
REVIEW
Analysing the experience. What could we do better next time? Where shall we go next?

Figure 4.4 The five stages of planning

just relate to an outdoor experience, they apply equally well to any project that we plan such as a school play or a family holiday. Although each stage merges into the one following, we should still be able to discern clear dividing lines between each phase. Many ideas for expeditions, proposed and discussed animatedly during a cosy evening in a pub, never come to fruition and, hence, never transcend the boundary between the concept stage and the planning stage; to use an analogy from the game Monopoly, they never pass Go! And quite rightly so; we should never attempt to curtail our aspirations and dreams, although what is possible with the resources and time we have available may make the practicalities rather different. However, once we begin to search out the relevant maps, investigate accommodation and locate equipment, we have entered the planning stage and the venture, as an entity, exists.

The concept stage

Communicating the objectives

Aram Bakshian (1996), one-time speech writer to President Reagan, writes that 'the difference between success and failure is the ability to communicate clearly and effectively'. Effective communication is one of, if not the most important, cornerstone of Outdoor Education. This is, of course, true in any field of human endeavour; within families, work or, indeed, life itself.

If we focus on communication within the context of Outdoor Education, it could be argued that, at its basic level, communication is simply a shared aim and the ongoing conveying of information in order to achieve that aim. An example of this may be a multipitch rock-climb where the aim is often simply to complete the route. The leader sets off, being belayed by the seconder from below, and the pair depend on established, and widely used, rock-climbing calls to inform each other of progress; 'that's me' shouts the second when the rope goes taught around him as the leader takes in the slack on establishing a stance at the end of the first pitch and who, once he has secured and prepared himself, replies 'climb when ready'. Commands are intentionally simple to avoid confusion and to allow a common code to exist so that one can adapt quickly to a new partner. At the other end of the communication continuum are major international expeditions where the necessity to articulate aims and objectives (especially to the press and potential sponsors on whose financial support the venture may depend) and communicate highly complex logistical requirements, is paramount to the success of the venture which can be severely jeopardized if one small issue is overlooked during the planning and preparation stage, or if the aims and objectives of the venture are not clearly communicated from the outset. Sir Chris Bonington cites an example of this when writing about the 1971 international expedition to Everest:

> The leaders wanted an expedition represented by climbers from all around the world, and they also wanted to make the first ascent of its massive South West Face. It then became evident that they had invited too many people for a single route. Not only that, many of the team members were not interested in trying a desperately difficult, unclimbed problem but wanted to be the first person from their country to stand on top of Everest and felt their best chance was by its easiest possible route. These different and opposing objectives led to conflict which undoubtedly contributed to the failure of the expedition to reach the summit by any route.
> (Bonington, 1994, p. 45)

At the level of youth work or school trips into the outdoors, effective communication from the outset is imperative and, indeed, is often a stipulated requirement of the local education authority. A clear understanding, among all parties concerned, about what educational outcomes it is intended to achieve from the experience, and what activities should be incorporated into the curriculum or programme in order to facilitate these outcomes, is fundamental. Everyone needs to know what they are going to do and why they are going to do it, and they need to have this information at the earliest opportunity, possibly during the concept stage and, if not, certainly early on in the planning stage of the venture. The objectives must be communicated, and they must be communicated clearly while there is the option of modifying, or even aborting, the venture before too much human investment, in terms of time and effort, has been expended. During this initial creative stage, the original idea is developed through investigation, discussion and brainstorming with colleagues until it becomes a concrete proposal, capable of being presented in written form (with the majority of potential questions already answered) to any agency responsible for approving the project, such as the school, youth service or local education authority, or interested in the project's outcome, such as the participants and their parents. It is through this process that our ideas become a reality and we enter the next phase of the venture.

The planning stage

Involving the parents

One of the recommendations of the *Report of the Altwood School Inquiry*, following the tragic death of four children on a visit to the Untersberg mountain in Austria during a school trip over the 1988 Easter holidays, was that: 'Information must be supplied to parents at an early stage in the planning so that they can make their decision on a properly informed basis and before being committed financially' (RCB, 1989, p. 23). The report appreciated that this would allow the possibility of parents refusing to allow their children to participate in the activity or trip, but stressed that this must be accepted. However, information is not necessarily the same as communication, and no matter how many professional-looking letters, brochures or packs we send out to parents we must ensure that the information contained in such worthy materials is truly communicated to the parents. In this respect, there is little to beat a series of meetings where parents can meet, face to face, the staff involved in the outdoor activity and where all the many nuances and details of the project can be clearly communicated between both parties. In this way, a dialogue can be established where parents will learn all about the trip and we, as leaders, may pick up snippets of information about the young people we will be taking away that, unless we had met their parents, we may have never known.

Such meetings also provide us with a crucial occasion on which the parents can verify that they have understood the implications of the activities in which their children will be involved. This, effectively, completes what should be a continuous loop of information–communication–verification. The parents can verify that any concerns they may have over the trip have been dealt with, and the leaders can verify that the parents have understood the full facts about the venture being planned, and that they, as leaders, have taken note of any parental input. I am not suggesting that we ask parents to swear on oath that the message has been received and understood, but the phraseology of the eventual letters of consent, which they must be required to sign to provide written permission for their child to participate, should indicate that they have attended open meetings, where the full facts of the trip were discussed, and that they understand the nature of the activities proposed. As such, we should be vigilant about ensuring that any parent unable to attend the set meetings has adequate other opportunities to meet with the staff concerned, even if this means an individual meeting at the parent's convenience. It may even be felt necessary to make it a condition of the child's involvement in the activity that their parent has attended a meeting (whether formal or informal) with staff. In the same way that many credit agreements provide a 'cooling off' period where the customer can change their mind, and not sign the agreement, once the initial – possibly ill-considered – enthusiasm for the purchase has waned, we should allow ample opportunity for the parents to find out all they need to know about the venture, to consider it at leisure, and to withhold their permission for their child to be involved if they are not totally satisfied about all aspects of the intended experience.

Professionalism

A further important aspect of communicating with parents at the pre-venture planning stage is that we, as providers of an outdoor experience, can maintain a professional approach to all we do. It is important, as in all sectors of education, for information to be presented accurately and comprehensively in a way which is convenient for our clients, the participants and parents, to digest. Nothing should be hidden from them. If there are to be periods of time during the venture when the young people will be unsupervised, which may be entirely appropriate for the experience we are providing, then inform them, in writing, that this will be the case and communicate with them at meetings to ensure that the implications of this are fully understood. There must, as we have seen earlier, be an atmosphere of client choice and a tacit understanding that, 'if you don't like it, don't do it'. It is taken for granted that participants and parents (on behalf of their children) must be allowed to opt out of the activity if there is any element about which they are less than totally happy.

The necessity for such a professional approach is a factor highlighted by the *Report of the Altwood School Inquiry* mentioned earlier which recognized that:

> Many parents have a greater expectation of teachers involved in an educational visit than they would of themselves. Teachers should be aware of the high standard of care required of them and their vulnerability. They must always be aware of potential hazards and, having made themselves aware, take the necessary safeguards. Adequate preparations will make any venture less stressful for the teachers themselves. (RCB, 1989, p. 22)

In effect, we should take the line that, although it is, of course, right and proper that parents themselves often make on-the-spot decisions about the level of freedom they allow their children (for example, allowing them to wander, unaccompanied, around a local town while on holiday abroad) it is only acceptable for us to allow the same freedom to the young people if we have informed the parents, in advance, that this will be the case. As seen in Chapter 3, we have a duty of care to ensure that we act responsibly at all times and this applies equally to the care we take in preparing and communicating as it does to the care we take while engaged on the planned activity in the outdoors. Hoyle and John (1995, p. 103), in considering the issue of professionalism, suggest that responsibility means that 'the practitioner's actions must ultimately be guided by a set of values which place a premium on client interests'. We must always remember that our charges are other people's children and it is, perhaps, the very fact that we have established such procedures for planning and communication that gives us professional credibility; the process leads to professionalism, and 'the difference between a true professional, and a merely competent amateur'.

Wheels within wheels

Although the total development of any venture is seen as a linear process (see Figure 4.4), rather than cyclical, as in the Kolb cycle, we must accept that there are cycles within each of the five key stages. This is especially true at the concept and planning stages where, as can be seen in Figure 4.5, each individual decision should always be seen as a cycle, and, thus, able to be reviewed and modified before the final solution is eventually settled upon. This may seem obvious, but there are many instances where planners have attempted to make the venture fit the circumstances, rather than attempt to find an alternative solution. No one factor can be viewed in isolation until all the many pieces of organization, which go to make up the final jigsaw of the venture, are in place and hence, some factors will require subsequent amendment because of the final decision on other issues. The whole planning process being, for much of the time, fluid and adaptable in nature.

Let us work though one simple example of this process: planning a ferry crossing for a continental trip. We may initially decide that, for the convenience of all concerned, the entire party

99

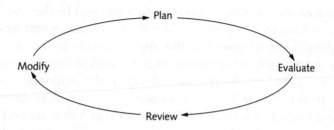

Figure 4.5 The planning cycle

should meet at the school at 8.00 a.m. on the day of departure, pack and leave by 9.00 a.m. and drive the three hours to Dover, arriving at 12.00 noon, to catch a ferry. We may then consult the travel brochures and discover that the only available ferry crossings that day depart at either 11.00 a.m. or 4.00 p.m. This leaves a problem to be resolved: do we attempt to leave earlier, and possibly inconvenience parents and staff; do we arrive at our planned time in Dover and hang around for a few hours; do we plan to make an educational visit or stop-off on the way to Dover; do we plan a later departure time to catch the later ferry; do we investigate a different route, from a different port or via the Channel Tunnel, which may possibly involve additional expense or longer driving time; do we say that the ferry does not fit our plans so we will go to Scotland instead? One thing is certain, we do not stick to our original meeting time of 8.00 a.m. and opt to rush the packing and then drive faster in order to catch the earlier ferry. Although it is the case that, in this example, we should have investigated the times of the ferry crossings as our first task which would have then dictated the time of departure from the school, we would still have been left with the problem of choosing between leaving school very early to catch the 11.00 a.m. crossing (in which case it may then become a better option to leave the night before and stay overnight nearer the port) or to leave later in the day which, in turn, delays our arrival and begins to impinge upon the time available for the venture.

As de Bono (1977, p. 53) says, 'a problem is simply the difference between what one has and what one wants' and many problems, some greater, some smaller, will be encountered during the planning stage of the venture and it is useful to have a process with which to deal with them. In the same way that we can encourage our young people to use problem-solving techniques to improve their decision-making, which will be discussed in detail in Chapter 6, leaders can develop their own methodology for approaching problems and decisions in a logical manner. Much has been written about problem-solving processes, and there are many models from which to choose. Doidge, Bone and Hardwick (1996) provide a useful illustration of a continuous improvement method used by quality teams, shown in Figure 4.6, which is as good as any in forming an approach to the planning of a venture.

Some problems or decisions may require a considerable amount of review and amendment before we settle on the final solution, while others may be more easily defined. If, for example, one of the early decisions we need to make is the maximum number of people we can take on the venture, we may be limited by factors outside our control. If only one minibus is available, we are effectively constrained by the number of seats the vehicle has. However, in our discussions and analysis of the problem, we may decide that a seat should be kept clear for use by a guide local to the area we are visiting. The number of participants we can fit into the minibus (the solution or outcome) is, therefore, restricted accordingly. We may, of course, wish to then invest-igate other means of transportation or of acquiring an additional vehicle, and we would use the process given in Figure 4.6 to take us through the decision-making process.

We must be careful, however, that we do not spend an inordinate amount of time, which is often our most important resource, in 'chasing shadows'. Much valuable time can be wasted in considering suggestions which never come to fruition, and not all problems we need to resolve will require the vigorous scrutiny as set out in the chart. As Doidge, Bone and Hardwick

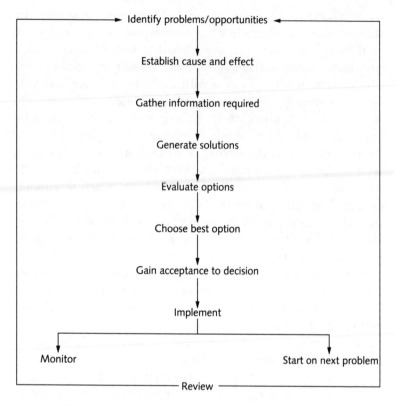

Figure 4.6 The problem-solving process
Source: Doidge, Bone and Hardwick (1996)

(1996, p. 10) state: 'There will be a need for some trade-off between time (as an investment to make an informed decision) and the need for a decision (for delay may sometimes be more damaging than a quick-fix).' It may also be that the exercise of formal data-gathering is not required in all cases as we are working within a set of predetermined parameters (such as the budget) which do not permit us the luxury of making totally free decisions about all aspects of the venture. This will, naturally need to be spelt out in the initial stages of the venture when we move from the concept to the planning stage.

Plate spinning

Now that we have found a methodology for dealing with the problems we will encounter, we should focus our attention on what problems and issues are likely to arise. At the start of the chapter, it was argued that Outdoor Education was 1 per cent perspiration and 99 per cent organization and this is because there is so much to organize and plan.

- *The group*
  The participants and their training or prior experience.
  Group composition (numbers, age, sex).
  The group's abilities (competence, previous experience).
  Pre-venture physical and mental preparation (training).
  Participants' medical history (medication and fitness to undertake venture).

- *Staff*
  Staffing and their qualifications.
  Hazardous activities and the supervision of them.
  Pre-venture 'recce' visits to the area/location by staff in advance of the venture.
  Liaison with local guides or outdoor providers.
  First aid qualifications of staff and medical arrangements.
  Qualified instructors; in-house (within LEA) or buy-in (centres, ski schools, etc.).
  Supervision and staffing levels (24-hour a day duty rota?).

- *Communications*
  Pre-venture information and communication with parents.
  Parents' meetings.
  Parental permission.
  School approval (senior management, governors, etc.).

- *Location and travel*
  The venue.

Accommodation (suitable for size and type of group/venture).
Transportation (train, minibus, etc.).
Travel arrangements.
Food and catering arrangements.
Local knowledge.
Language (spoken and visual communication) if an overseas venture.
Foreign currency and methods of payment.
Evening activities and alternative plans.

- *Safety*
Emergency procedures.
Contact points throughout the venture.
An alerting cascade.
School, youth service or local education authority (LEA) requirements and guidelines.
Medical and health questionnaires from participants.
Compliance with regulations under the Adventure Activities Licensing Authority.
LEA or national youth organization guidelines and regulations.
Governing body regulations (for hazardous activities).
Risk awareness and documented assessment.

- *Administration*
Finances.
Documentation (including passports, visas, E111, minibus documentation, etc.).
Travel insurance and breakdown cover/recovery.
Personal belongings insurance.
Activity insurance (mountain rescue/personal accident).
Record-keeping (financial, medical, etc.).

- *Equipment*
Group and personal (purchased or loaned).
Specialist equipment hire (hire locally to home base or at destination).

The list is seemingly endless, and they all have to be planned at much the same time. No wonder it feels, on occasions, as if we are a circus act spinning plates on sticks; forever throwing another new plate up into the air and then rushing around frantically keeping all the other plates spinning at the same time. Even the above list is deceptive as each item covers a multitude of individual tasks to be planned and performed. Before we can plan what we are going to organize, we should take some time to look at the vastness of the task. To do this we shall, for a worked example, focus on a necessary aspect of many ventures, the provision of a minibus.

On first impressions, it may be thought that all one has to do is borrow the school's or youth service's minibus, but it is not as simple as that. We have a duty of care to ensure that our organization of the venture is watertight, and that means checking, and providing documentary evidence that we have checked, all aspects of the transport arrangements are in order. It has been said that the most dangerous thing about many youth expeditions is the minibus which gets you there, as it is an unfortunate fact that the consequences of a minibus crash are infinitely more disastrous, in terms of injury and human life, than the number of fatalities occurring in the hills. Although modern legislation, requiring forward-facing seats with individual seat belts, has improved matters since my first journey to cub camp packed, along with all the gear, into the back of a removal lorry, that same legislation has placed a moral responsibility on us as leaders to ensure that all legal requirements and safety precautions relating to the vehicle are met. Many of the ventures with which we may be involved are, by their very nature, dependent on travel. Some require travelling to mountainous or wild country areas, and the more ambitious may even involve journeying outside of the UK. There will, therefore, be a myriad of details concerning the minibus to be organized, under this one aspect of the venture alone, some of which are illustrated in the cascade diagram in Figure 4.7.

We can see from this diagram that there are progressive tiers

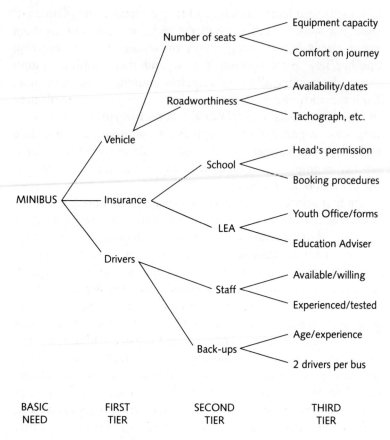

BASIC   FIRST   SECOND   THIRD
NEED   TIER   TIER   TIER

Figure 4.7 Minibus cascade

branching out from the basic need to provide a minibus. At the first tier we have the three fundamentals; we need a vehicle, the insurance and other paperwork to legally allow us to use it, and people to drive it. Each of these three then subdivide into the second tier: the number of seats the vehicle has which will limit the numbers of participants we can accommodate; the roadworthiness of the vehicle and its MOT; whether it is the school or local education authority who deals with the insurance, especially for overseas trips; are there sufficient members of staff approved by the school or LEA as drivers, and do we have back-ups in case one of the designated drivers falls ill?

The illustration in Figure 4.7 only shows three progressive tiers of issues to be raised and confirmed; there could, of course, be many more. Some basic needs such as equipment, may have considerably more tiers and it will also depend upon individual circumstance; not all the branches of the cascade will eventually be of the same length. The benefits of this system are that it can be tailored to individual needs. The system provides a tool for ensuring that we 'do not leave any stone unturned' during the planning process and, if we have ticked all the aspects we have identified, it provides proof of the thoroughness and professionalism of our planning. The other main advantage is that developing this system is not time critical in that we are considering a process, rather than a specific venture, and can, therefore, consider many of the various issues well in advance of starting to plan any one particular project. It will mean that, once we have produced cascade diagrams for all our basic needs (given in the list at the start of this section) we have the methodology firmly in place to adapt these to each project we subsequently plan. Sometimes we may not need one aspect of the process. If, for example, we have decided to travel by train, we will not need the 'minibus cascade'. However, we shall need to produce a similar diagram of our chosen travel arrangements to ensure that no aspect is overlooked.

Critical mass

The use of this cascade method of identifying issues allows us, as leaders, to undertake several other extremely useful project management techniques within our planning cycle. First, and most simply, we can, with the help of such diagrams, view the outdoor experience or venture, in whatever form it takes, as an entity and can begin to look at its overall size in terms of the demands it will make on the planning time available. We can extrapolate, having identified all of our basic needs and from producing a diagram similar to Figure 4.7 for every such requirement, that the planning for a venture could become increasingly more complex until it reaches its critical mass, in other words, being the largest it could become and still be manageable by one person. At that stage, rather than stretch ourselves too far and attempt to undertake an impossible workload, we could draw in the assistance of other people to organize certain aspects of our venture. For example, one person may take on the organization of the minibus, while another takes responsibility for equipment. The cascade diagrams then become, in effect, important communication tools in allowing us to convey to others the scope of their duties and an easy way for them, in turn, to demonstrate progress. The technique can also be used, just as easily, by the young people themselves when, if they are involved in a self-led peer group venture, the group may deliberate over the production of cascade diagrams for each area of need and then each individual may take responsibility for arranging one aspect of the project (such as the food, or the equipment) before they all pool their collective efforts as a group exercise.

Critical path analysis

The second important technique we can employ is a well-known tool in project management, that of critical path analysis. If, after we had produced our cascade diagrams, we were to take a highlighter pen and mark over each diagram following the conclusions at which we have arrived, we would, in effect, have produced an illustration of the critical path that we must follow in order to reach our desired outcome, in this case the provision of a minibus and drivers. We could then use the diagrammatic representation of this path to consider where potential stumbling blocks may occur. For example, if there is only one minibus available within the local education authority, it would be wise to check whether it would be available for use during the proposed dates of our venture, and provisionally book the bus, before we get too involved in finding drivers and other such details, as it may be that our potential pool of drivers is different, because of local authority regulations such as age, depending upon which vehicle we use. If the local authority requires an internally organized minibus driver's test to be taken by all drivers, we are limited by those members of staff who have completed such a test, whereas hire companies may stipulate that all drivers must be over 25 years of age, which gives us a different subset of possibilities. However, if we have identified this potential problem in our critical path analysis, we have the time to ensure that the situation is resolved by ensuring, if necessary, that any potential drivers undertake the local authority's test well in advance of the venture.

Critical path analysis is, fundamentally, concerned with ensuring that all functions which, collectively, make up the total project, are undertaken in the correct priority, or chronological, order. Professions such as civil engineers are practised exponents of the process as if they are, for example, building a flyover, they must ensure that the steel framework is ordered, delivered, constructed and erected, and that the concrete is laid and dry, before the road-surfacing materials and road-rollers arrive. It would not be efficient, in terms of time, effort and money for there to be piles of surfacing materials and machinery on site waiting for other stages of construction to be completed and, following a continual process, they only need the paint and the painting equipment for the white lines in the middle of the road once the surface has been laid and has set.

A way of adapting this into our planning process is for all staff involved to brainstorm all the tasks that need to be undertaken and then arrange these tasks in order of priority. Examples of this technique can be found in many management training manuals and variations on the theme include writing each individual task on one of the ubiquitous yellow sticky office notelets which can then be stuck to a wall or large table and rearranged during discussion.

The movable crux

Once we have identified our critical path, we can employ another useful technique, which I have termed the movable crux. This, again, is nothing new, but a technique taken from the computer industry and applied to our planning process. When installing a complete integrated computer system into an office block, the engineers will analyse every function which has to be undertaken, from installing the wiring to ordering and delivering the actual machines. They will then determine which of these functions is potentially the most difficult and which will cause the most problems; this is then the aspect of the installation they attempt first. In other words, rather than undertake all the various tasks in a set chronological order, they do the most difficult part first. This may, at first sight, appear slightly contradictory to the concept of critical path analysis where a continuum of tasks is set in priority order. However, the notion of a movable crux is, in effect, a process within critical path analysis as it encourages us to look at the complexity of each individual task and prioritize it within our overall planning path.

To follow the example of civil engineers constructing a flyover, it may be that, although they want the road-surfacing materials to arrive on site after the steel skeleton has been built and clad in concrete, the actual manufacture and processing of the surfacing material requires the longest lead-in time of any component in the project. The project managers would, therefore, need to ensure that the road-surfacing materials were ordered, as a priority, early on in the critical path of the project so that work on other aspects would be under way while the surfacing was being manufactured.

This considered sequencing of priorities can be likened, as can be seen in Figure 4.8, to rock-climbing where routes are graded by the difficulty of the hardest move, the crux. Often this crux move is in an exposed part of the route which has taken much effort to reach and where the consequences of failure will have the most serious results. If we could move the crux to the very beginning of the route a great many factors would then be to our advantage. We would be able to attempt the move while we were fresh, without expending effort just to reach it. The consequences of failure would not be so severe and, if we did fail, we could attempt it again without wasting considerable time and effort. Finally, once we were over the crux, we would know that the rest of the route was easier in comparison. Moving the crux in this way is obviously impossible to achieve on natural rock, but it serves as an analogy to show what we can do with logistical problems in our planning cycle. Although it is true that a crux is an impediment wherever it occurs, we can, by moving it logistically, lessen its potential negative impact and ensure that margins, or buffer zones, of time are in place around the crucial points of our planning.

Let us compare this notion of the movable crux in planning to a possible example in organizing an overseas expedition. As we move from the concept stage to the planning stage, we draw out our cascade diagrams of all the various basic requirements for which we need to plan, one of which is the documentation necessary for overseas travel, such as visas and travel permits. We then consider all the diagrams and highlight any which must be prioritized as they will seriously affect the operation of the venture if they are not completed in time for our scheduled departure. One such would, of course, be entry visas to the countries we intended to visit. We can, then, ensure that we apply to the various embassies in plenty of time for our visa applications to be processed and returned while other components of the planning are taking place concurrently. How much better than organizing the whole venture only to discover, in the last couple of weeks before departure that visas are required. Again this may appear simplistic and patronizing to suggest that any competent planner would overlook such a detail; it is not meant to be. It is merely using a planning process as a tool to ensure success without stress! In any event, circumstances can often wrong-foot us and it has been known for expedition

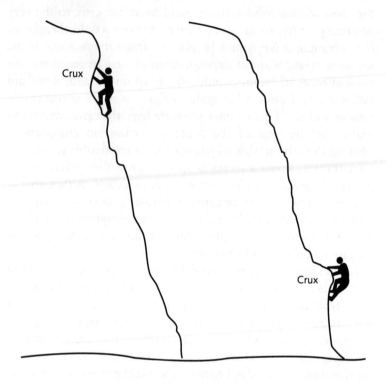

Figure 4.8 The movable crux in planning

groups comprising members of different ethnic backgrounds to find that, as some held passports issued by countries other than the United Kingdom, a small minority of the group's members required visas for certain countries to be visited during the expedition while the remainder did not.

The transition to reality

We have seen, so far in this chapter, how various processes and methods can be implemented to aid us in our planning prior to the venture itself. Ideally, at some stage, we accept that our planning is as near complete as is possible and decide that the venture can begin. However, the reality is often that the prep-aration for the venture continues right up to the moment of departure which is often a date preset many months in advance. This we must accept, although it cannot be emphasized enough that, as long as our planning cycle has been in order, and we have ticked all the appropriate boxes to verify that we have completed all the necessary details, the fine-tuning of our prep-arations will of its own accord 'expand to fill the time available' right up to the last possible second. At that point we cross over from the planning stage to the action stage of the venture when the breadth and depth of our planning is put into operation.

There are many excellent publications available to help leaders through the maze of planning, such as *Educational Visits* by Julie Smart and Gill Watson (1995) and *Leading and Managing Groups in the Outdoors* by Ken Ogilvie (1996). The HMSO publication *Safety in Outdoor Education* (DfEE, 1995) provides much helpful advice and extremely useful appendices such as a draft parental consent form, recommendations on emergency procedures and a checklist for the conduct of out-door education activities. It is certainly worth the effort of taking a little time at the beginning of the planning stage to undertake a search of the available literature and to review the advice of others. After all, to use a hackneyed phrase, there is no point in reinventing the wheel!

The action stage

Every action has a reaction

This chapter is concerned with the planning for an outdoor experience and, as such, must look in detail at the events which are likely to occur during the venture. It must be stressed that, for the ease of continuity, this next section will cover areas which will be put into effect during the venture itself, although they would, of course, have been organized during the planning stage.

Everything which occurs during the venture, if all goes according to plan, should be the result of input from the leaders. This implies that nothing which occurs during the venture, barring accidents or incidents outside our control, should take us by surprise as nothing should happen which has not been previously considered and planned for. We should also plan for the unexpected. This is not a contradiction as, even if the unexpected does happen, we should have a system in place to deal with it!

Putting the plans into operation

We have, earlier in this chapter, looked at how we must liaise with the school, youth office, local education authority and parents at the planning stage of the venture to ensure agreement with our intentions. It was stated then that it was communication, rather than simply information, which was required. Once the venture is under way, the information we leave behind is a vital part of the communication link between the venture and the home base, and it is important that due thought and consideration is given to this area. Many local education authorities will have their own requirements concerning off-site trips and it is important that any leader checks with these requirements in the first instance. However, we should aim to work at a level of best practice which can clearly demonstrate that we take our responsibilities as leaders seriously and, to this end we should, ideally, provide parents with a comprehensive pack of information about the trip so that they are fully briefed, in writing, about all aspects of the venture. This pack should be completed sufficiently ahead of the venture's departure for it to be handed to parents at an open meeting so that they can talk through every detail and ask questions as they arise. It may be decided by the school or youth group that this information can be posted to parents or delivered to them by their children. In which case, it would be sensible to send a full accompanying letter providing contact phone numbers for parents to use if they require additional information. It may also be felt necessary to have a reply slip for the parents to sign and return indicating that they had received the information pack.

It is suggested that such a pack should contain, as a minimum, the following information about the venture:

1 A copy of a letter of authorization from the school or LEA, signed at the highest possible level, giving permission for the trip to go ahead.

2 Details of any/all vehicles being used on the venture including: make, model, registration number, number and type of seat and what kind of seat belts are fitted. Names of designated drivers and back-ups. A list of all participants who will be travelling in each vehicle (if there are multiple vehicles being used, it is recommended that participants and staff are allocated to one particular vehicle throughout the trip so that, if a vehicle was to become lost *en route* or there was to be a crash or other incident, it would be easy to determine exactly who was in the vehicle).

3 Details of the communication arrangements between the group and home base for the duration of the venture.

4 The emergency communications procedure which will be followed by the group, school, youth service and LEA in the event of an incident.

5 An outline of the procedure which will be put into action should a member of the group not return to a rendezvous point at the specified time while on any unaccompanied visit during the venture. This should outline what action the participant should take and what action will be taken by the party leaders. This should be carried at all times by the participants on the venture.

6 A comprehensive timetable/itinerary for the trip showing all relevant dates and times (i.e., departure and arrival times).

7 The plan of programmes for each day of the venture, including travelling days, providing a complete breakdown of all specialist activities to be undertaken and any periods

during which the young people will be unsupervised. Ideally, each day would have a page of its own, even if this means repeating some information.

8 A list of all the staff, their qualifications and experience, involved on the venture. If external staff are being utilized at any stage in the venture (local guides, ski instructors, etc.) their details or, if this is not possible, at least, information on the organization to which they are affiliated (mountain centre, local ski school, etc.).

9 Contact address, telephone number and nature (hostel, camping, etc.) of each night's accommodation.

10 Copies (for their information) of any forms, such as the parental consent form and a medical history form, which they, as parents, have been required to sign.

This information should be clear, concise and factual. The overall impression which the parents have of the venture, and their professional regard for us as leaders, will be significantly enhanced by the clear indication, through the information we send to them, that the venture has been thoroughly and carefully planned.

We should also supply the above information to all the staff and young people participating on the venture as well as to the school, youth office or local education authority. The information provided to these officers in positions of responsibility should include the following additional items.

11 Checklist of all staff and participants on the venture.

12 Emergency contact numbers for every person. The information provided to the school or youth office should include copies, in confidence, of the medical/emergency forms which provide a contact address for everyone throughout the duration of the venture.

13 A breakdown in diagrammatic form of the alerting cascade which will be put into operation should something go wrong, and written procedures which will be followed.

14 A checklist for each minibus showing what items should be carried and used, such as tachograph (if applicable), insurance documents, green card, driving licences, warning triangle, first aid kit, spare bulbs, etc. Comprehensive and up-to-date advice on this is best sought from one of the national motoring organizations.

15 If the venture is travelling abroad, participants should be issued with a letter explaining exactly what they are doing and where they are going. This letter should then be translated into the language of every country which the venture will be visiting or journeying through. In the event of a participant being separated from the main party, the appropriate translation can be shown to someone in authority, rather than the participant struggling to converse in a foreign language.

As the above information is designed for use by the participants while on the venture, some thought should be given to its layout and presentation. It is doubtful that the participants will feel inclined to carry an A4 folder around with them all the time, whereas a smaller brochure may fit into a pocket. Some groups may even have the facility to laminate some of the vital information into plastic covered cards which are less likely to be damaged and can be carried around more easily.

A communication link

However thorough the information we provide to parents, they will often, quite naturally, be keen to receive occasional progress reports on the venture, especially if it is of a long duration or to a foreign country. A prudent leader will arrange, during the planning phase, to be in regular contact, ideally daily by telephone, with an office or staff member at base (the home contact) so that parents calling the school or youth group can obtain up-to-date information on the venture. This should apply even if it is known that there will be regular contact by phone between the young people and their parents, and if the contact number of the expedition base has been provided to parents in advance. Having one 'official' link alleviates the tendency for 'Chinese whispers' to evolve where distorted stories of events find their way home only to become embellished as they are retold between parents or friends.

As leaders it is important that we do not view the establishment of such communication links as being in any way negative or an intrusion into the venture we have planned. Communication is a two-way process, and it has certainly been known for such links to convey vital information out to the group as well as from the venture back to home. One such case is an extremely unfortunate event where the parents of a child on a venture were involved in a serious road traffic accident and the predetermined communication system, between the party leader and the school, enabled the child to be returned home with little loss of precious time.

Modern technology has taken communications into a completely new era and this has, naturally, had implications for expeditions and not all of it for the better. At the negative end of the scale there have been reports from rescue organizations of walkers who feel that a mobile phone, on which they can summon immediate help should they get into difficulties or become lost, can compensate for basic navigational skills and adequate equipment. Stewart Hulse (1995), from the Langdale and Ambleside Mountain Rescue Team claims that 'people decide that they don't have to learn about maps and compasses, the weather or route planning. They think that if they get into trouble all they have to do is dial 999'. At the extremes of outdoor adventure, mobile phones, satellite links and, even, faxes and e-mails have kept the modern explorer in touch with their home base from the worlds highest mountains, widest oceans and remotest arctic wastes. It is a quantum leap in technology from the time it took to learn of Captain Scott's ill-fated expedition to the South Pole in 1912, to the mountaineer Rob Hall whose last known act, before he tragically died on

Everest in May 1996 was to call his wife, at home in Christchurch, New Zealand, on his mobile phone. As Jim White (1997) said, in an article on the modern hi-tech explorer, 'nothing can be worse than being in touch but beyond rescue'.

While the above two examples are not part of the outdoor activities with which we are involved, they illustrate how communication is constantly changing and it is not uncommon for leaders of youth expeditions to keep in touch with each other, and home base, by mobile phone. Indeed, used correctly, mobile phones are very significant benefits in terms of safety.

The alerting cascade

The establishing of an effective communications link through a home contact has a further important dimension in the provision of an alerting cascade, and many youth services and local education authorities will already have guidance for the provision of such a system within their Outdoor Education guidelines and regulations. The system involves deciding in advance what action, with regard to informing home base, should be taken if something remiss happens to the venture or any member of the group. It is difficult enough, if something goes wrong (even if it is only a case of industrial action at a foreign port delaying an intended return date) without trying to cobble together a method of contacting the school, local education authority or parents. An alerting cascade provides a preplanned method of contacting the maximum number of people in the minimum time. A designated person, usually the headteacher or outdoor activities adviser for the LEA, is crucial to the implementation of the cascade and it would be this person whom the expedition leader calls in the event of a mishap. This one person calls a number of prearranged others who, in turn, call a planned list. Many local education authorities and voluntary youth organizations also include regulations on speaking with the press in their guidance on action after any form of incident as it is vital that the established facts are communicated through one, officially designated, source. This is often the local authority or head office press officer, and it is vital that staff leading ventures or trips are familiarized with these procedures as a matter of course and that copies of any such policies must be taken on the expedition by the leader. An example of an alerting cascade is given in Figure 4.9.

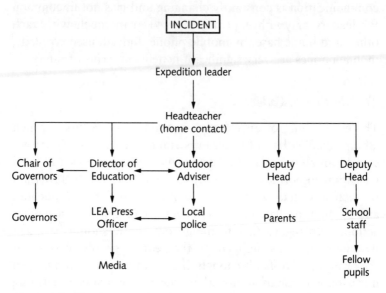

Figure 4.9 An alerting cascade

Record-keeping

Apart from ensuring that the venture adheres to its plans, the leader of any venture must be especially fastidious about one other function throughout the duration of the experience and that is keeping records. This is an important matter as recording all events which take place during a venture reinforces our professionalism and provides evidence of all our actions.

Some records are obvious. If we have young people who are on prescription medication, it is reasonable in many circumstances for the parents to request that the staff look after the tablets and ensure that the correct dose is taken each day by the child. If this is the case, a medication book should be established containing a page for each child outlining the nature, dose and frequency of their medication and then a record of it being administered, at the correct dose and frequency, by a member of staff. It is important that there is an element of confidentiality about this process, as some children and their parents may not wish all the other participants to know details of their medication. Even if the children are responsible for administering their own medication, on an as need basis, such as with asthma inhalers, it may be that the leaders will feel it prudent to look after a spare inhaler in addition to the child's. This should also be recorded, and carefully labelled, so that there is no confusion over ownership in the haste which surrounds a child having an unexpected attack of asthma. Similar records apply to any personal items which the leaders look after on behalf of the participants: valuables, passports, spending money. All should be carefully logged and recorded, even to the extent of the child signing out their valuables and spending money so that there can be no future doubt as to the correct administration of their belongings.

Other records are not so obvious. The complete history of any illness or ailment suffered by the participants, even if it is as apparently innocuous as an insect sting, should be recorded. Times, symptoms and descriptions could be important factors later if the child suffered any allergic reaction to the sting and a history of the symptoms was required in order for a hospital or doctor to make an informed diagnosis. Likewise, if a participant suffers any minor injury which requires first aid, the exact treatment given must be recorded. This is an example of good practice which can be learnt from procedures carried out at Outdoor Education centres where records provide a vital back-up to safety. For example, it is common practice for equipment usage to be recorded. Ropes will be numbered and each will have its own personal history recorded. It will then be inspected after each period of use and cut up after a certain number of uses or a certain period of time. At Outward Bound centres, for example, details of all accidents, illnesses, aggravated injuries and near misses are compiled and categorized (as either minor, significant or serious) and analysed annually at a local and national level. This record-keeping ensures that trends or activities that produce a high proportion of incidents are identified.

Records also have an important contribution to make at the review stage where the information they contain may provide useful insights valuable for the planning of future ventures. This is especially true of any financial records which should provide a comprehensive breakdown of all income and expenditure so that audited accounts of the venture are available for inspection by the parents at the conclusion of the venture.

The reflective stage

Making sense of the experience

It should be stated that, in many cases, the reflective stage is as important a part of the educational process of Outdoor Education as the venture or activity itself. This is the part of the venture where the participants review the experience, recognize and share the learning outcomes, and re-live the memories. Reflection allows us all to internalize the experience and make it a real part of our continual educational progress. Many organizations, such as the emergency services who encourage the development of critical incident debriefing skills, have incorporated reflective practices into a systematic approach aimed at getting the most out of all events, as the techniques apply equally to understanding, coping with and improving on any negative issues as they do to enhancing the positive aspects.

The concept of reflective practice originated with *The Reflective Practitioner: How Professionals Think in Action*, by D. A. Schön (1983) and much subsequent research has been undertaken into the subject. Boud, Cohen and Walker (1993) consider reflection as a generic term for processes involved in exploring experience as a means of enhancing understanding.

An opportunity for reflection should, therefore, be built into any outdoor experience, no matter how short, as it enables the participants to get feedback from their peers and the expedition's leaders and to identify what learning has taken place. Armed with this key information, they can approach the next opportunity with increased confidence and ability. The notion of feedback is an important part of much current management development practice where it can take several forms. Polly Kettley, a research fellow at the Institute for Employment Studies and author of a report entitled *Personal Feedback: Cases in Point*, states that when feedback comes from subordinates it is upward appraisal, when it comes from subordinates, peers and the line manager it is personal feedback, and when it comes from all these sources it is termed 360-degree feedback. Polly Kettley (quoted in Coles, 1997) maintains that: 'Feedback schemes are especially suitable for measuring behaviour related to leadership and relationships . . . the perceptions of the people you are working through.' This is a useful concept as, for the majority of cases in Outdoor Education, where the whole group along with the leader will often review experiences and reflect on the outcomes, 360-degree feedback is commonplace.

The Reflective stage is, therefore, a vital part of the total experience of Outdoor Education and should be planned and designed to enable participants to recognize that all ventures and outdoor experiences have the dimension of an intellectual or emotional challenge as well as the physical challenges. In many cases, involvement in an outdoor experience will be demanding on the body's physical reserves but it is right and proper that the activity should also provide a mentally challenging and stimulating experience. For the young people, as indeed it is for us as leaders, an outdoor venture is a chance to be away from the thoughts that occupy us during our everyday lives, to concentrate solely on the task in hand and deal with what the elements throw at us. It is also a time when we are away from the comforts of home, and share with our fellow group members the emotions and feelings that arise from our undertaking. The venture provides opportunities for personal and social development, as well as educational progress, and often it is when friendships are consolidated and a group is formed, from a collection of individuals, which can share the common memories for years to come. Every group's experiences are so similar, yet each is totally unique.

As part of the planning which we, as leaders, undertake towards the venture, we should prepare ourselves and the participants both physically and mentally for the challenge of the experience, much in the same way as sports competitors begin preparing towards an event many weeks, and even months, beforehand until they reach peak performance levels. As well as physical training, runners will also rehearse in their minds every second of a forthcoming event, riders and drivers will visualize every detail of the track or circuit and team players will analyse the opposition, mentally recording every detail of their opponents, and 'psyching' themselves up before a big game. This can also be applicable to our ventures and expeditions where we can benefit from thinking through all the details and demands of the project so that tension and anxiety will be considerably lessened once the venture is under way and we are putting our long period of organization into effect.

This approach is especially apt for the young people. They will have been looking forward to the venture with mixed feelings of excitement, anticipation and, if exhilarating and potentially hazardous pursuits are involved, perhaps a little trepidation. This is very healthy, and we can all benefit if such feelings can be recognized and recorded by the young people themselves after the venture so that they can begin to appreciate what they have gained from the experience. The reflective stage of the venture is when we can to draw out the responses, feelings and emotions of the young people to the experience they have recently been through and we must recognize that we have to plan for this crucial part of the overall package in the same way as we have planned the rest of the venture. It will not just happen by accident.

There are many simple tools which we, as leaders, can utilize to facilitate an effective reflective stage. However, we must remember that we are not attempting to be amateur psychologists, rather, we should aim to guide the participants towards a realization that there is much more to an outdoor experience than the activity itself. They have a unique opportunity to consider how they interact with one another, what their own personal feelings were while they attempted a challenging activity, how they perceive themselves and how others perceive them. As we have seen above, Outdoor Education is as much a mental process as a physical one and it is through this stage of the venture that both facets of the participants' personalities are strengthened. Ideally, the reflective stage will be where the participants open up in discussions with the leaders and talk through all that occurred during the venture. This is a considerable task, both for the participants, to remember everything that took place as, often, events are seen in retrospect 'through rose-tinted spectacles' where the good aspects are embellished and the bad points gradually forgotten, and for the leaders who may require 'prompts' to stimulate discussion and reflection among the group. The following suggestions may help both sides in achieving a meaningful outcome and, hopefully, should be seen as enjoyable, non-threatening, activities rather than anything intrusive.

Chuff charts

The chuff chart, a well-established group work technique, is simply a piece of card with the x and y axis of a graph drawn on it. Along the bottom (the x axis) is the duration of the expedition marked off into appropriate intervals; every hour may be too much, every two hours should suffice, as it is, of course, possible for participants to have a different card for each day. Up the side (the y axis) is a simple score of 1 to 10, with 10 being very good and 1 being very bad. All we do is mark on our own individual chart how we feel, on the score of 1 to 10, at the various intervals. Leaders should produce these charts in advance of the venture, during the planning stage, possibly using a different colour of card for each day of the venture or residential experience. The cards need only be small, A6 or A5 at the largest, as the technique aims to provide a quick and easy way for participants to record their feelings. Each card should provide a space for the individual to enter their name, the date and the activity being undertaken. An example of a chuff chart is shown in Figure 4.10.

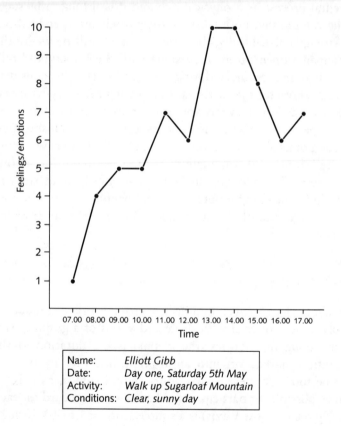

Name:	*Elliott Gibb*
Date:	*Day one, Saturday 5th May*
Activity:	*Walk up Sugarloaf Mountain*
Conditions:	*Clear, sunny day*

Figure 4.10 A chuff chart

When the outdoor experience is over, or at the end of each day, the participants can plot a graph from the points they have recorded and show how their feelings were fluctuating up and down over the duration of the venture. When each individual's chart is compared with those of the other members of the group, we may find that they all felt very 'down', and scored low numbers, at certain specific times and we can try to remember what caused this. For instance, it may have been a long hard slog uphill in the rain with little visibility. On the other hand, we can also identify when all the group felt good or elated, perhaps, for example, an exceptional view when they stopped for lunch, and we can plot exactly this point on the map of our journey. It may be, however, that one member of the group was feeling elated by the slog uphill and scored a 9 when everyone else marked down 1 or 2. It is, of course, also possible to combine all the charts on to one bigger chart showing every group member (perhaps in a different colour) over the period of the venture, to show how the group, collectively, felt and to indicate any similarities or large differences. We could also take all the results at each hourly interval, add them together and divide by the number of people in the group to get an average, and plot this as a general, anonymous, chart of the group's overall feelings.

If we do find, for example, that two members of the group have very different scores on their charts for the same moment on the venture, we can discuss where they were at that particular moment in time. We may find that the group were attempting abseiling for the first time and that, although trained and qualified staff from an outdoor centre were instructing the activity and full safety equipment was being used, the perceived risk, to one participant, overshadowed the enjoyment factor and they scored 1 on their personal chart. Another member was exhilarated and full of adrenalin and scored 10 on their chart. The important factor to draw out from group discussion is that two people who were in exactly the same place, at exactly the same time, experienced such differing feelings over exactly the same activity. Some critics of Outdoor Education will argue

127

that it is too activity based to be a valid developmental tool for working with young people, yet it is through the skilled debriefing of the participants' own feelings over such activities, that we can begin to appreciate the views and opinions of others. Surely it is only a short step from discussing the participants' differing feelings while abseiling to reflect, for example, on the feelings of two individuals from differing ethnic backgrounds or cultures being in the same place at the same moment in time.

The results obtained from such charts do not, in themselves, actually prove anything and are thus totally non-threatening to the participants; they are not exposing their innermost secrets, but expressing a feeling at one particular moment in time. All it does is to allow the group to reflect, in a simple manner, impressions of how they were feeling at any one time. These discussions could move into the wider aspects of the venture: why there were vast differences between the scores of various group members on some occasions and why there was total agreement at others. We could even combine the results of the chuff charts with a map of the venture and transfer the groups points scores on to the position on the journey when they were recorded, although this would require advance planning as someone would need to make a note of the grid reference or location each time the group marked their charts. This, accompanied by photographs taken at the same time, would give a fascinating insight into the group's experience over the duration of their expedition.

Action charts

We can use exactly the same technique as the chuff chart for the group to record many other aspects of their venture. As well as intangible aspects of the venture, such as their feelings, they can record tangible aspects such as each individual's physical contribution to the activity, who was doing what at various intervals; who was using the map, or chatting, or joking, or moaning, or eating. From this data, with input at the reflective stage from the leader, the participants themselves can identify and discuss what they each, individually, gained from the experience, and consider issues such as who among them seemed to be the natural group leader, or the morale booster, or who was inclined to be the navigator.

By recording feelings and events on chuff charts and action charts participants get a very real impression of the underlying group process and can appreciate, tangibly, each other's strengths and weaknesses. They may also have gained an impression (rather than a deep psychological perspective, as such charts are only simple, largely superficial, tools) as to the interpersonal relationships within their group. With the addition of photographs and other personal memories from the venture, these results also provide a basis on which a very real reflection of the project can be made, possibly to those at school or youth club who were not able to participate on the venture.

Self-concept and perceived self

The idea of basic charts to record thoughts, feelings and emotions during expeditions or other ventures can be used in a variety of ways. They can be used to look inwardly at ourselves, to observe others, and even to chart how we believe others are perceiving us. A similar method can be put to work to determine, in a rudimentary way, any changes in how people view themselves; what is sometimes called their 'self-concept'. This, however, requires some prior planning as the first chart needs to be completed by the individuals concerned as soon as they begin their involvement in the venture at the planning stage.

A simple grid can be produced, as in Figure 4.11, with opposite traits and personality characteristics on each side. The participants themselves, possibly as a group, could decide these traits, and much discussion may ensue from attempting to find a balancing counter-characteristic.

The words within the chart are not, in any way, intended to be on a good/bad basis in a moral sense, but merely aim to point

129

DEPENDABLE						UNRELIABLE
OUTGOING						WITHDRAWN
RELAXED						STRESSED
GREGARIOUS						SHY
HARD-WORKING						LAZY
OUT OF SHAPE						PHYSICALLY FIT
DEPRESSED						CHEERFUL

Figure 4.11 A self-concept chart

to certain characteristics. The participants as a group should be encouraged to think of as many pairs of contrasting words as they can, and then refine the list until they are happy with it. This is not intended to be a sophisticated diagnostic process, rather a simple tool for making the reflective stage of the venture more meaningful, so it does not really matter if some of the words, or characteristics, chosen appear to overlap with traits which are already included on the list. It is more important that the young people feel a sense of ownership about the exercise.

At the very beginning of the planning stage, when the venture or expedition itself is still a long way off, the leader should ask each participant to fill in two charts: one for how they see themselves (their 'self-concept') and the other for how they think the other members of the group view them (their 'perceived self'). All they do is put a tick or cross in the box between the two opposing characteristics which they feel applies to them. For example, in Figure 4.12, the person sees themselves as very hard-working, although they think that others may feel that they are inclined to be a little lazy!

Once all the group have completed the two sets of responses, the leader should lock the papers away so that the individuals concerned cannot look at them again. Later, during the reflective stage, when the group has completed the venture (usually some

Self-concept

HARD-WORKING	X				LAZY

Perceived self

HARD-WORKING				X	LAZY

Figure 4.12 Example of self-concept and perceived self chart

weeks, if not months, later) they should be asked to fill out exactly the same two forms once again. This will mean that each member of the group will have responded to how they see themselves and how they feel others view them both before and after the venture. Retrieve the original forms which the group filled in at the beginning of the planning stage and, as part of their personal reflective process, ask them to highlight any differences in the two forms they have completed. We may find that, originally, a participant saw themselves as lazy but now, several months and the challenge and communal experience of the venture later, see themselves as more hard-working. The leader can encourage the group to discuss among themselves whether there been a great deal of change and, if so, what has changed most, the perceived self or the self-concept? Did all the members of the group have similar changes?

These results, again, do not prove anything in themselves, but they will provide a springboard for interesting group discussion. Some may be able to put forward reasons why they feel that the experience of completing the venture has altered the responses they made. Others may say that it had nothing to do with the project itself but that they felt differently about themselves because their examinations were a year nearer, or they had recently begun college, or started a job, or perhaps just because they were another year older! Everyone's contribution to the discussion is valid, as what one person may see as being a positive effect, others may view as negative. No one is right or wrong, but a good debate or written critique could form the basis of an excellent formal reflection not just of the final venture, but of involvement in the whole process leading up to it.

One note of caution, however. We don't want the group to be so concerned with looking inwardly at themselves that they forget to enjoy and appreciate the experience of completing the venture. Too much analysing of one's own feelings can lead to introspection and consequently to missing the wonders the expedition or venture has to offer. It is probable that we are more likely to have feelings of joy and happiness when we are not analysing and looking inwards, but looking outwards! Although feelings and emotions are important, and we need to be aware of them in ourselves as well as in others, especially, perhaps, on any form of residential experience, too much emphasis on the individual may not necessarily be a good thing. We must remember that the vast majority of outdoor experiences require young people to interact with their peers and that the group dynamic and team-building qualities that Outdoor Education can offer are some of its major contributions to personal and social development. The opportunity to appreciate our own strengths and abilities, as well as developing a regard for the vital contribution of others, is a facet which benefits from practical experience in the field and young people should be encouraged to view their personal experiences in relation to the experiences of others. As has been said, the whole is worth more than the sum of the parts.

5 A team or a collection of individuals? Exploring team-building in Outdoor Education

Gangs, tribes and teams are, in many respects, all the same; what we want are teams.

HRH The Duke of Edinburgh

Introduction

Over the last decade, everywhere we look, industry and commerce and the general world of work appears to have gone mad on the notion of teams. Offices and businesses have, internally, regrouped their staff from departments or centres into teams. We have credit control teams, customer care teams, project teams and, even in education, there are teaching teams and curriculum design teams. Considerable research has been focused on the subject and new concepts such as 'quality teams' and 'super-teams' promote current best practice. Godfrey Golzen states that new ideas about management generally originate in America or Japan, but that Britain has led the field in recognizing the important contribution that teamwork can make to business success and suggests that this is because of our traditional preference for team sports. He quotes Paul Thorne, an industrial psychologist, who, in supporting the view that teamwork is becoming more important as the nature of work changes, says that 'management is no longer about running an assembly line of sequential processes, but about giving assignments to groups of people committed to bringing them to a successful conclusion within a specific time. It's like winning a game' (Golzen, 1993).

133

This approach has certainly caught on and, at the top end of the scale, multinational corporations have utilized teams to take forward new product design or to investigate how their services can be improved. This team culture has led to interesting spin-offs such as the examples of 'bubbles' and 'skunk works' quoted by Hastings, Bixby and Chaudry-Lawton (1986). A bubble consists of a few people interested in pursuing an idea for any improvement to a company's products, services or organization:

> Once the bubble is given the go-ahead, people in it are paid extra for working in it but are expected to do their everyday job as well. The management accepts that most bubbles will probably burst, but sufficient new ideas, innovations and motivation come out of them to make gains far outweigh the losses. (*Ibid.*, p. 7)

Skunk works, used by the company 3M in the USA, are 'small groups taking an idea, taking it forward if it looks to have a potential, but dropping it quickly if it shows no promise' (*ibid.*). Reorganizing into teams seems to have become a universal panacea for all organizational ills.

All this has, over time, filtered down through the system until 'teamwork' seems to be at the top of every employer's want list from prospective employees. Recruitment advertisements stipulate 'outstanding team player required' while a sub-headline in *The Times* of Monday 25 March 1996 stated that 'Universities put teamwork skills on wanted list'. But what exactly are teamwork skills, and what is a team? Even in what is, perhaps, the most commonly accepted definition of teams, within sport, the terminology can be confusing. At a basic level, there is considerable variation of the number of members which a team contains: rugby union has fifteen, rugby league thirteen, there are eleven in soccer and six in volleyball, four make up a 100 metres relay squad, pairs play bowls and doubles play tennis. When is a team not a team, or is it possible to have a team of one – or one thousand?

John Adair states that a team is more than just a group with a common aim. He feels that a team is a group in which the contributions of individuals are seen as complementary, and that collaboration is the key feature of teamwork. Adair (1986, p. 108) proposes that an effective team is one where 'its members can work as a team while they are apart, contributing to a sequence of activities rather than to a common task which requires their presence in one place and at one time'. Although this seems like a contradiction to the concept of teams in sport, it could also be seen as an extension, as sports teams are, in reality, only together and focused on the task for a small percentage of the time. They do, of course, maintain a fixed aim and identity even when they are not together and, although collective training sessions are important for tactics and working together, individual skills can be practised alone and in isolation by the team members, contributing to a sequence of events which could be their fixture list or even a number of successive seasons.

The same can apply to groups or teams planning an outdoor experience. As we saw in Chapter 4, the planning stage can often be spread over many months and individual members of the group can be engaged in important tasks, vital to the eventual success of the venture, away from their fellow members. In terms of teamwork, Sir Chris Bonington (1994, p. 46) sums up the planning stage of the venture as being 'the period when the culture of the expedition is established. In involving as much of the team as possible in the work of organisation, each having a role and job, you are building up a sense of involvement and commitment'. However, Bonington acknowledges Adair's view that the team can contribute to a sequence of events even though they may be apart:

> Until the team sets out everyone has been scattered, leading their every-day lives at the same time as taking their part in organising the venture. They might have come together for the odd weekend, but their separate day-to-day lives will have been dominant. (*Ibid.*)

Team-building as opposed to team games

One feature of educational debate over the 1980s and 1990s has been the issue of competitive team sports in schools. Apart from the teaching unions' industrial action in schools during the early 1980s, which broke the habit of teachers giving up time outside the curriculum to coach teams, there has been, at one extreme, psychologists calling for a ban on team games such as soccer and rugby in schools, branding them 'macho' and suggesting that they only serve to encourage aggression. This body of opinion led many schools, especially those in the primary sector, to drop competitive sporting fixtures and focus on individual exercise instead of team competition. At the other extreme, an MP has occassionally called for the return of competitive sport to restore self-discipline in the young. Iain Sproat, minister at the Department of National Heritage responsible for sport, was quoted in the *Guardian* as saying:

> When I talk about sport in schools I do not mean step-aerobics, going for country walks and listening to lessons on the history of diets. These are all right in their own way, but they are not what I want. I want team games properly organised – competitive team games, preferably those which we invented, such as soccer, rugby, hockey, cricket and netball. (Pilkington and Moss, 1994)

The same newspaper article also reported Mr Sproat as stating that 'If we had more organised team games in schools, we'd have fewer little thugs' (*ibid.*), which prompted John Evans, professor of physical education at Loughborough University, to respond that 'Sport has as great a capacity for producing bullies and thugs as it has good citizens and saints' (*ibid.*).

Professor Evans's view has recently been supported by research undertaken by scientists from the University of Otago in Dunedin, New Zealand. Dorothy Begg, from the university's Injury Prevention Research Unit, writing in the *British Journal of Sports Medicine*, counters the belief that young people's aggression can be safely channelled through sport and states that their study 'does not support the view that involvement in sporting activity is a panacea for delinquent behaviour; if anything it indicates that it may exacerbate the problem' (quoted in Mihill, 1996). The Otago research suggests that, although it has been traditionally believed that sports build character and that, by participating in organized sport, young people are exposed to strong conforming, rather than deviant, influences and thus become good citizens, the alternative view is that involvement in sport encourages aggressiveness and even cheating, which can, unfortunately, be successful in games. In today's mass media world, examples of cheating within international sport are widely observed, such as the Argentinean footballer Maradona's infamous 'hand of God' incident in a World Cup match against England. The Otago report states that 15-year-olds with high levels of participation in sport were twice as likely to be delinquent at 18 years of age than their less sporty counterparts. Although this chapter is not, in any way, intended to be critical of school sport, the interesting factor of the Otago research is that they conclude that outdoor activities, which provide individual challenges, are likely to be more effective in helping young delinquents than organized games.

This is neither new or surprising as outdoor adventurous activities have long been used by social services as part of their work of intermediate treatment with young offenders, subject to supervision orders imposed by magistrates' courts, where, in addition to taking part in activities designed to develop confidence and self-esteem, participants are introduced to ideas of co-operation and teamwork to provide them with important social skills to enable them to find appropriate employment away from delinquency and petty crime. In one such example, in 1995, the Home Office announced a grant of £430,000 annually, for three years, to the youth-orientated charity Fairbridge to finance four-week residential courses for young offenders which included activities such as mountaineering, sea-canoeing, potholing and orienteering, as well as community work like road-building and helping disabled people. Baroness Blatch, Minister of State at the Home Office, was reported as saying that such courses would 'motivate young offenders, through learning new skills and self-discipline, to be responsible and law-abiding. Tough and challenging physical activity, opportunity for acquiring new skills, for working with and learning from others are all part of this important initiative' (Ford, 1995). It seems that such courses are aimed at transforming young offenders into team players within society at large.

Management and development training in the outdoors

In addition to young offenders, Outdoor Education has, since the inception of the Outward Bound movement in the 1940s, been used to promote teamwork, communication, problem-solving and other important skills to commerce and industry as part of development training programmes. Alongside the proliferation of commercial providers aimed at this market, the Institute of Management introduced, in 1993, its own outdoor management development course as it recognized that the outdoors, for developing skills such as leadership and the application of effective teamwork to problem-solving, provides a rich arena for experiences which are memorable, stimulating and enjoyable. The courses focus on team-building as the Institute believes that, if managers can work as a team during the course, they will work better still back at the office. A popular view is that, as firms become smaller and less hierarchical, they need to build more effective teams. Deborah Brown, human resource manager at the Stock Exchange, was quoted in the magazine *Personnel Today* as endorsing this view, 'It's no longer good enough to be average. As organisations get smaller, they have to be efficient and use everyone as effectively as possible. Team working creates more synergy and boosts performance' (Haughton, 1993, p. 23).

There are many parallels to be drawn with the use of Outdoor Education with young people, and a simplistic question would be to ask, if industry and commerce put such store in teamworking and invest considerable funds in outdoor training and consultancy, why do we not use exactly the same techniques with our young people through existing programmes of extremely financially viable Outdoor Education to give them a competitive headstart in the employment market? This becomes a more obvious strategy the more one reads into industry's use of such training, where, in common with the reflective stage of the venture discussed in Chapter 4, considerable emphasis is placed on reviewing activities. Jane McCann, training and development consultant for Allied Dunbar, again quoted in *Personnel Today*, puts this into a business perspective:

> outdoor learning is good fun and gets people together on the same level, but it's hard to take what you've learnt back to work on Monday. You need to spend more time afterwards consolidating it – one problem for us was not doing enough of that. (*Ibid.*)

In the same magazine, Suzanne Neville from the Industrial Society, reinforces this view: 'Debriefing is the most important element of a team building activity. People seldom review group processes, how people interact with each other – effective teams regularly review these things' (*ibid.*, p. 30).

Business has also found that the way that an employee reacts in an outdoor situation, away from the office, illustrates their natural tendencies and personality. Mike Sewell, a senior consultant at KPMG was quoted in the *Sunday Times* as endorsing this view, 'in challenges away from the workplace, people fall into their natural roles and the physical dependence on other members of the team to accomplish a given task brings the lesson of teamworking home' (Golzen, 1993). In the same article, Mike Meldrum, who runs one of Cranfield School of Management's short courses, of which outdoor activities are an integral part, supports this perspective by suggesting that 'when you take people out of the office environment and put them under unfamiliar pressures, they revert to type' (*ibid.*). If this statement is true, and classification of an individual's personality type provides a useful indicator as to their potential work-related performance, we should consider various methods of assessing such personality traits which, again, has been a fertile area of research. Psychometric testing, also called psychological tests or occupational tests, plays a large part in modern recruitment procedures and, in an Institute of Personnel and Development survey undertaken in 1994, 85 per cent of personnel directors said that they used personality or aptitude tests as part of their selection procedures. But what do such tests discover, and how is this of concern to us with regard to Outdoor Education?

Personality types

All teams have members of varying personalities; the emotional creative genius or the steady stalwart. Recent research by George Sik and Stephen Smith, presented to the British Psychological Society conference at City University, London, studied professional footballers by using a questionnaire designed to seek information on personality types and found that: 'The players who survive in the game are the more caring, tolerant and interested in the welfare of others. They are also more forward-planning, more interested in other players, why they behave as they do, and more co-operative' (quoted in Hawkes, 1995). To continue this sporting analogy, one consistent feature of sports teams is that individual players are often assigned positions on the team sheet, but it is the role they undertake as part of the game plan which distinguishes their task (this is, of course, with the possible exception of the goalkeeper, whose title and task are pretty much synonymous). Dr Meredeth Belbin, in *Management Teams: Why They Succeed Or Fail*, noticed that this applied equally to business teams and suggested that a team is not a bunch of people with job titles, but a congregation of individuals, each of whom has a role which is understood by the other members.

Through his research at the Administrative Staff College at Henley, Oxfordshire, Belbin analysed hundreds of teams until he had identified eight categories of functions which he maintained that the individual members performed. Belbin believed that members of a team seek out certain roles and they perform most effectively in the ones that are natural to them and suggested that an ideal team included one person undertaking the role of each of the following categories (Belbin, 1983, p. 78):

1 *Chairman*
Calm, confident, trusting; a good chairman; clarifies goals, promotes decision-making; strong sense of objectives.
Not necessarily the cleverest or most creative.

2 *Plant*
Creative, imaginative, unorthodox, individualistic.
Bad at dealing with ordinary people; inclined to disregard practical details or protocol.

3 *Shaper*
Dynamic, outgoing, highly strung; challenges, pressures, finds ways round obstacles.
Prone to provocation, irritation and impatience.

4 *Teamworker*
Social, mild, perceptive, accommodating; listens, builds, averts friction, promotes team spirit.
Indecisive in crunch situations.

5 *Completer/Finisher*
Painstaking, conscientious, anxious; searches out errors; a capacity for follow-through; perfectionism.
May worry about minor details; reluctant to delegate.

6 *Company worker*
Conservative, dutiful, predictable; practical common sense, hardworking, self-disciplined; organized.
Lack of flexibility; unresponsive to unproven ideas.

7 *Resource investigator*
Extrovert, enthusiastic, curious, communicative; explores opportunities; responds to challenge.
Liable to lose interest after initial enthusiasm.

8 *Monitor evaluator*
  Sober, unemotional, prudent, strategic, discerning. Sees all options, makes judgements.
  Lacks inspiration and ability to motivate others.

It has been said that the value of Belbin's analysis is that it outlines the weaknesses as well as the strengths of each member of the team and this is of potential value to those of us working with young people who, if choosing one of Belbin's nine categories as being that which suits their personality, can be encouraged to begin to explore their failings as well as their strengths. Interestingly, Belbin makes a category specifically for 'teamworker' although it could be argued that all individuals should, to a greater or lesser extent, be teamworkers and fit into the overall team no matter what their individual personality, skills or contribution.

In a more light-hearted vein than Belbin's categories, other popular examples of classifying people into personality types have likened individual characteristics with animals: the rhino, who is thick skinned and disinterested; the ostrich, who buries his or her head in the sand and refuses to face reality or admit that there is a problem, and the owl, who looks very solemn and pretends to be very wise, using long words and complicated sentences. Although they lack the intellectual depth of Belbin's work, such analogies to animals may be a way of initially introducing the concept of personality types to young people as the approach is potentially less threatening, especially if they themselves were to allocate characteristics to various animals.

More seriously, Dr Howard Gardner (quoted in Mihill, 1995), from Harvard University, has identified what he believes to be seven different types of intelligence:

- Spatial intelligence
- Logic
- Language
- Music

- Kinetic or bodily intelligence
- Social intelligence
- Interpersonal intelligence

Dr Gardner has researched seven acknowledged geniuses reflecting each of these areas. Freud (interpersonal), Einstein (logic), Picasso (spatial), Stravinsky (music), Martha Graham (kinetic), Ghandi (social) and Eliot (linguistic). An interesting facet of Dr Gardner's research is that none of the seven geniuses he has identified, with the possible exception of Picasso, showed any indication of their success before the age of 20 and that each carefully selected the area that best reflected their abilities once they had reached adulthood.

Whether one uses Belbin's personality types, or Gardner's classifications of intelligence, it is important that a successful team contains a mixture of people contributing a variety of different skills. This is especially true in any major expedition. Sir Chris Bonington, writing about the fundamental principles which make teams function successfully, refers to planning the successful 1975 Everest South West Face Expedition:

> Having worked out the basic logistics of the expedition, I had a sound idea of how many people I needed and the kind of skills I required. This didn't mean I wanted only good climbers. I also needed organisers, people who would be happy to fulfil a support role, and those with specialist skills such as medicine, communications and so on. (Bonington, 1994, p. 46)

Bonington also appreciated that personality types, as well as key skills, were important:

> Even among the lead climbers there had to be a combination of temperaments. I didn't want a team of prima donnas, but equally I didn't want a team of passive people. It was a matter of getting a balance between driving forceful characters and ones of a more supportive nature, and being confident that they would all work within the structure of the team. (*Ibid.*)

This again shows how useful classifications such as Belbin's personality types could potentially be as it provides a way of ensuring that we obtain a balance of varying skills and temperaments within the overall team. This is summed up nicely, using, once again, a sporting analogy, by Ian Hutchings, writing in *The New Academic*, who looks at the notion of whether specialists are more valuable than all-rounders:

> How does a Premier League football club achieve excellence? Certainly not by recruiting a team of all-rounders. Success is built upon the encouragement of teamwork, the recruitment of specialists (a striker if the team's goal scoring record is weak; a better goalkeeper if the ball ends up in their net too often), and getting the right blend in the team. A first-class side does not reach that eminence by expecting all its members to be good at everything – no club drops an outstanding goalkeeper because he fails to score any goals! (Hutchings, 1993, pp. 1–2)

A breakdown in teamwork

The success of any team will depend on the strengths and abilities of the people within it, although those very strengths and individual characteristics may, occasionally, also lead to disharmony. Individuals' differing personalities have a far-reaching effect on the group dynamic, and much research has been undertaken on what happens when teamwork breaks down. Minor, and sometimes not so minor, disagreements and differences of opinion or view are a common feature of all teams; in a very real and important sense, it is exactly this continual refocusing of perspectives that forms and binds a team together, a gradual consensus of view from a collection of individuals. However, a breakdown in teamwork, especially in an established team, is very serious and, just as they illustrate so many other things, major expeditions can provide classic examples of what takes place when this happens. The breakdown in communication which occurred between Sir Ranulph Fiennes and Dr Mike Stroud while on an unaided expedition to walk across Antarctica in 1993 has been well documented, not least because each man wrote and published a personal account of the venture which detailed problems of teamwork. Stroud, in his book, called one chapter 'A Question of Leadership', revealing tension over who was the leader of the two-man team.

However, what allows this particular expedition to show that the intense pressures of such a demanding venture provoked emotional flare-ups between the two men was the fact that they had worked very closely together while undertaking three previous expeditions and that, some few months after the Antarctic venture, they had, apparently, re-established their friendship. In a newspaper article published at the time that the two explorers' books came out in print, Ed Douglas of *Mountain Review* was quoted as saying that antagonism between compatriots in such a situation was normal:

> In such conditions a natural antipathy builds up. You are hitting your reserves of physical energy all the time; coming up against barriers of your own self and trying to beat these barriers. When two very competitive men are involved, rivalry is inevitable. (Lennon, 1993)

This view was supported medically by Dr Thomas Stuttaford, writing in *The Times*, who compared the experiences of Sir Ranulph and Dr Stroud with hostages and submarine crews:

> When active, competitive people are kept in hazardous and cramped surroundings, every personal characteristic can create tension; their tone of voice, their laugh, conversational gambits, ways of eating and even their smell. It requires great detachment and self-control for someone not to conceal their own natural fears by projecting them as feelings of anger about companions' characteristics. (Stuttaford, 1997)

We may all have seen a very much milder form of such situations on many residential trips with which we have been involved because, as Dr Stuttaford implies, any grouping of individuals will highlight differences in personality, views and actions. Our job, as responsible outdoor educators, is to manage such situations sympathetically to ensure that they do not become out of control with the result that any one member of the group feels isolated from the remainder. It has been said, however, that what has come to be termed 'positive discontent' within teams is an effective way of stimulating continuous improvement and, although this may well be so when considering design teams and the like in industry, where discontent, expressed intellectually rather than personally, at aspects of the enterprise may be in pursuit of perfection in the development and manufacture of the product, rather than disharmony among colleagues, it may not be the case with young people engaged on an expedition or teamwork project as part of an outdoor residential as any discontent within a team can become, ultimately, very destructive to both the team and the individuals concerned.

It should be noted that, as we saw in Chapter 2, many youth organizations have programmes of outdoor training, within their overall framework, which are developmental in nature in terms of providing thorough training prior to the final venture or experience. As well as building on the participant's growing maturity and increasing skills, the period of training and practice trips, allows opportunities for the young people to form themselves into a group and, more often than not, 'moderate out' excesses of behaviour on the part of any individual, which considerably lessens the possibility of later conflict within the team.

Leadership

We saw, above, that the role of chairman rather than that of leader was identified by Belbin as one of the leading roles necessary for a successful team. This may be the case within an expedition group when the leadership may rotate around the members of the group depending upon which task has to be performed. Considerable research has been done on the subject of leadership and many books are available which, especially those by John Adair (1986, 1988, 1988a) mentioned in the Bibliography, are well worth reading as sources of information.

Professor Adair states that certain functions have to be performed in order to meet the three 'areas of need' of the team. These three areas of need are: a) to achieve the common task, b) to be held together or to maintain themselves as cohesive unities, c) the needs which individuals bring with then into the group. The functions which have to be performed are

- Awareness (of what is going on in the group)
- Understanding (knowing that a particular function is required)
- Skill (to do it well enough to be effective)

However, Adair questions whether these are membership or leadership functions, or, in other words, should every member of the group or team perform these functions or just the leader? Professor Adair makes the point that it is often better to talk about leadership rather leaders and that leadership resides in the functions not in a person. Therefore, the group could share leadership among themselves and leadership would pass naturally from person to person.

The exercise of allocating personality types to members of the group, undertaken before the venture, could be combined with a refined version of the action charts, mentioned in Chapter 4, modified to record exactly who was undertaking which role at various times throughout the duration of the venture. During the reflective stage the group could cross-check whether the Belbin roles which were assigned to group members prior to the expedition matched up with how they actually performed during the expedition. It would be interesting to note how these roles fitted in with the idea of having a team leader and whether the group found that they did, in fact, need an identified leader or whether decisions during the venture were made entirely by group consensus.

The concept of rotating leadership within an expedition group is very similar to the management development training notion of 'self-directed teams' which suggests that the leadership of the team moves naturally to the person most able to lead specific parts of the overall task. However, this has the possible danger of leaving a leadership vacuum, especially if no one person is obviously better equipped than the others in the group to lead a certain aspect of the project and no one is prepared to push themselves forward. George Davies of Cambridge Management Centre has been quoted as saying that 'You need someone to set the goals, to maintain a sense of purpose and direction. Otherwise they [teams] can become committees, where things get discussed rather than done' (Golzen, 1993). However, leadership from within the team can have advantages, especially when the group are involved in potentially hazardous outdoor activities where, as we saw in Chapter 3, there is an element of risk. The UKMTB in *National Guidelines* (1995, p. 14) suggest that leaders need to be able to anticipate the possible risks involved in using particular environments and state that 'Risks will be minimised if leaders are familiar with members of their group, their strengths, weaknesses, person-alities and previous experience.'

Rotational leadership, and many other facets of the group's interaction, can be discussed and considered during the reflective stage, as long as this has been planned from the outset. Using the various techniques mentioned in this section, participants could be encouraged to produce recorded observational data illustrating when and how various tasks within the group were passed from one individual member to another and which particular task was being carried out at any one time. The group themselves could then discuss whether they felt the need to have a nominated leader for certain tasks outside the actual expedi-tion itself such as, for example, arranging informal planning meetings before the venture to discuss the food or equipment that they would take with them. If the group felt that it was important for them to have someone acting as a nominated leader, could they decide to have a different leader for each day of the expedition? Should this involve functions such as ensuring that the group were up and out of their sleeping bags on time every morning, and that the campsite was free of litter? Or should the group perform these tasks among themselves as a matter of course? It may be that a group needs an enthusiastic start in the mornings to bring them out of their warm tents to face another day, and that this could be rotated around the group. It is known for expedition groups out for several days to take it in turns to be first up, light the stove and provide the rest of the group with a cup of tea in bed. By sharing such activities equally, each member of the team shares, fairly, the benefits and disadvantages. But is this leadership, or purely a task? Will Carling (quoted in Austin, 1993), a recent England rugby union captain, saw his role as motivating the other members of the team to ensure that they all performed to the best of their ability. A hot cup of tea to start the day, without even getting out of your sleeping bag, sounds, to me, like pretty good motivation, and it may be that, rather than having one person continually trying to motivate the expedition team, simple activities such as this can ensure that the team motivates itself.

Many scenarios for discussion could be set to the group prior to the venture to ensure that all the above issues were considered and that the concept of leadership was fully clarified within the team. How do the group feel about having a leader in case they have an accident on the hill? What happens if it is the leader who is the casualty and cannot, therefore, exercise their role? Should every member of the group be capable of assuming leadership of the group at any given time? Has a natural leader emerged during the period of training? Does the group need a leader after the venture to ensure that reports of the journey are completed?

Putting the theory into practice

What can be done then, in terms of developmental team-building, if we are to meet the general requirements of industry and society to produce young people who are rounded team-workers? Outdoor Education is, by its very nature, often concerned with group activities (although, of course, it is

149

possible that individual participation in an outdoor activity may be part of an overall programme). It provides us, therefore, with an ideal vehicle to encourage young people to look at themselves as part of a team, each member of which contributes an important part towards the success of the whole.

Group dynamics

Techniques such as the chuff chart outlined in the reflective stage of the experience in Chapter 4 can be adapted and used to allow individuals to record what their fellow members of the group 'do' during the venture or experience. We can formalize this and, through looking at and discussing what each individual does, begin to form an impression – or analyse – what the exact role is which they are performing within the group. Each member of the group has a role, whether this is consciously acknowledged or not. Are individual members of the group interchangeable? Could the 'navigator' become the 'motivator' and vice versa? Or is it the unique personality of each individual which influences which role within the group they perform?

Consider each member of the expedition group. Are the Belbin personality types, or the characteristics they represent, present within the team? There are nine distinct categories according to Dr Belbin, but often a much smaller number of participants within an expedition group. Which roles are left out, or are some doubled up? Are each of the roles necessary for a balanced expedition team? All roles within the group are equally valuable and mutually complementary, and the good navigator may attribute the success of the venture to the group member who kept morale high, while the 'morale booster' may say the success was due to the good navigator never getting the group lost. While this teamwork occurs in every expedition – or, at least, in the great majority – it is often hard for the young person involved in the experience to acknowledge it happening.

We could, therefore, encourage each member of the group to identify which of Belbin's types they feel they fulfil and, similarly, to allocate a role to each of the other group members. Is there general agreement between the individual and the group over each member's 'type', or do people see themselves as being one type of team member while the rest of the group see them in a different light? This could link in with the suggestion of looking at self-concept and perceived self considered in Chapter 4. It should be emphasized again that we are looking at overall indications of personality types, traits or characteristics with our young people and not, by any stretch of the imagination, attempting to undertake full personality or psychometric tests such as those used in recruitment. Such tests should only be used by trained practitioners and the Institute of Personnel and Development issues a code of practice as to their use.

Dr Belbin's eight categories were, through the focus of his research, primarily aimed at looking at teams within large business organizations and it may be that our groups of young people could consider whether they feel that the categories which Belbin identified are appropriate for an expedition group and whether they themselves could decide which categories to omit or to see if they can think up other categories not already covered. Any new categories could be given a name and general attributes and shortcomings, as in the list, and the group could attempt to identify these characteristics among their peers.

Team-building

Once we have encouraged individual members of the group to think about how they see themselves, and how they feel others perceive them, we can introduce the notion of looking at the building and performance of a team. The group, to successfully complete the task of undertaking their venture, should perform as a team. They come together at the beginning of the planning stage as a collection of individuals but, through the process of training and preparation, they gradually form together as a team. We can begin to help them realize that they have formed into a functioning unit, to contemplate their strengths and

151

weaknesses, and to visualize how others may view them as a group. Will they be perceived as a happy team enjoying their expedition, or a rather dour group carrying out a chore? Do they feel that their campcraft is well organized – with each member of the group having a definite role – or is it slightly chaotic with tasks being performed on an *ad hoc* basis? Is their preparation and route-planning efficient and neatly presented, or is it all left until the last minute?

Team charts, similar to the self-concept chart outlined in Chapter 4, can be produced with various categories and descriptions, as in the examples in Figure 5.1. Other headings such as; Morale, Planning, Teamwork and Cooking can be thought up by the group themselves to investigate every conceivable aspect of their performance.

This technique can be used over the duration of the total experience to show whether the group themselves feel that they have improved their performance over the course of their involvement and are working as a team. It will enable them to identify their individual as well as collective strengths and weaknesses and to take steps to improve any aspect of their performance about which they are not happy. It can also help them to look forward to the final venture as a group exercise rather than an individual effort.

Perhaps, if the school, organization or youth centre has two or more groups undertaking a training programme at the same time, different groups can repeat the exercise for each other so that they have an outsiders view of how they perform. The trainers and leaders could also complete the same charts as the group themselves and the difference of opinion could be discussed. It may even be that the participants could use the same technique to evaluate the instruction given to them by the trainers. Were sessions clear, understood, in too much depth or not enough? The 360-degree feedback discussed in Chapter 4 should not apply only to the participants.

CAMPCRAFT

SAFE					DANGEROUS
COMFORTABLE					MISERABLE
TIDY AND CLEAN					MESSY
ORGANIZED					CHAOTIC

NAVIGATION

EFFICIENT					HAPHAZARD
ACCURATE					ERRATIC
TEAM EFFORT					INDIVIDUAL
SAFE					DANGEROUS

Figure 5.1   Team chart examples

Problem-solving

Another interesting aspect of the group's mental approach to their venture is how they respond to critical moments on the expedition when they are required to confront a very real problem. Although this will be covered in greater detail in Chapter 6, the notion of problem-solving cannot help but overlap into team-building, as a multitude of events, throughout the duration of the venture, will require the group to exercise their collective problem-solving abilities.

At each point there will, naturally, be several different opinions from different members of the group as to how exactly to deal with the problem. How does the group decide which action to take? Is there fair and 'democratic' debate, or is a more random and arbitrary decision made? Does the quality of debate change at different stages of the venture: when the weather is bad, or when group members are feeling tired and irritable? All these are problems which the group solves as a team, so can we introduce to the group the notion of brainstorming as a way of solving problems which arise *en route*? This is a commonly used technique within the context of teamwork and problem-solving, and is advocated by John Adair (1988a) in *Effective Leadership*. The process works by encouraging people to deliberately suspend judgement, to refrain from criticism and to think of as many ideas – or solutions to the problem – as possible. Instead of attempting to immediately identify the correct solution to every problem, encourage all members of the group to throw in as many ideas or suggestions as possible. Each one can then be discussed on its own merits by the group and accepted or rejected until the best possible solution is found.

If one member, throughout the venture, adopted the position of an undercover reporter, or 'passive participant observer' as we could term the role, and noted down the decision-making process which the group adopted, how long discussion lasted, who contributed the most, who said the least, etc., every time the group confronted a problem-solving situation, this could lead to a fascinating account of the venture. Some groups have actually been quick enough to photograph themselves as they struggled to erect the tent, or after one member has accidentally trodden in another's dinner. What appeared to be major traumas at the time are often the most treasured memories afterwards.

Self-evaluation and evaluating the group experience

Although we have looked, very superficially, at the psychological impact of Outdoor Education, the venture should not be about trying to encourage participants to become amateur psychologists! Rather, it should offer ways in which young people can – possibly for the first time ever – offer some meaningful evaluations of themselves rather than having someone else do it, which is what largely happens at school or college. The process is an important one to learn, and is a valid learning experience. It is very interesting for the group members themselves to recount how they feel they have performed, rather than the leader expressing an opinion as to the performance.

Involvement in Outdoor Education can be a turning-point in a young person's psychological development and, by using a few simple techniques such as those outlined above, we can encourage them to make the most of the experience. We would not be maximizing the potential of our young people if we merely allowed them to mechanically take part in an exciting outdoor experience without stretching every aspect of their personality.

6 Learning to expect the unexpected: A problem-solving approach to Outdoor Education

> Mankind always sets itself only such problems as it can solve;
> since, looking at the matter more closely,
> it will always be found that the task itself arises only
> when the material conditions for its solution already exist
> or are at least in the process of formation.
>
> Karl Marx, *A Critique of Political Economy* (1859)

Introduction

It is, I believe, a popular misconception that Outdoor Education is a totally physical pursuit. The average person, if asked to describe their perception of what is encompassed by educating in the outdoors, will all too often speak of the physical exertion of climbing mountains, the demands of cross-country skiing or the fitness required to canoe or mountainbike off into the wilderness. Although it is true that physical fitness plays an important part in the enjoyment of outdoor activities, the use of the outdoors for educational purposes should be equally as concerned about the mental development of young people, and we have already seen, in Chapter 4, how important the cerebral aspects of the venture – such as evaluation, review and reflection – are to the overall whole. Successful Outdoor Education is a mental, as well as a physical, process.

For example, even the more extreme outdoor activities rely on mental, rather than purely physical, agility. Paragliding does not require great physical strength. More important in deciding whether a teenager is mature enough to try flying free from the rope is their decision-making capability. Tom Beardsley (1994), the British Hang Gliding and Paragliding Association's Safety and Development Officer, states: 'Every youngster can experience fear. They must be mature enough to understand and remember instructions and retain that understanding in a dangerous situation. For instance, gusty conditions could drive instructions out of their minds'.

Although self-discovery, or self-directed learning, and an investigative approach feature highly in modern classroom teaching, although not without their critics, conventional education is often more concerned with imparting hard facts which form a knowledge base for each individual subject. Two plus two will always equal four! However, we, as outdoor practitioners, combine the teaching of hard skills necessary to undertake an activity such as climbing or skiing – in effect, our knowledge base of facts – with the imparting of an approach or attitude towards the subject, the soft skills, which often encompasses intangibles such as environmental and spiritual awareness, self-reliance and, as we saw in the previous chapter, teamwork, leadership and the like. The most important of these soft skills is, I believe, the development in our young people of a problem-solving approach which Outdoor Education does so much to inculcate and which is, through the development of the skills of collaboration, communication, critical reasoning and making informed decisions in demanding situations, so valuable to a person's continued intellectual and cognitive development.

It has been argued, perhaps in an oversimplistic way, that conventional education teaches us, by and large, how to deal with the expected: Outdoor Education teaches us to deal with the unexpected; to 'problem-solve' our way across difficult terrain, to deal, if necessary, with an emergency which we hope we will never encounter.

To expand this theme further, I am going to focus on wild-country foot expeditions to illustrate the 'holistic' approach to physical and mental development which is, I believe a cornerstone of Outdoor Education. This, to some extent, continues the theme raised in Chapter 2 of the importance of the unaccompanied foot expedition within Outdoor Education as being a way in which young people, within a controlled framework of safety, can truly take responsibility for their own actions, with very real and meaningful consequences. As *In Search of Adventure* states:

> The second condition which reinforces the impact of Outdoor Adventure experience for the young is that, as far as possible, they should be able to exercise choice, make decisions and solve problems with minimum interference from accompanying adults. It is obvious that, in any situation which involves an element of physical or psychological danger, adults have a great responsibility; the penalty for mistaken judgement can be high. (Hunt, 1989, p. 163)

Once the hard skills of navigation, campcraft and the like, so vital for the successful completion of a foot expedition, have been mastered in a training setting, we begin to focus on problem-solving concepts such as 'what to do if you get lost' to give participants the decision-making skills they will need if they are going to complete a journey in wild country on their own. Trainers tend to lapse into this approach quite naturally and some would even include it under the heading of the vital hard skill of navigation. However, I believe that it is more complex than that. We are beginning to teach an approach; an attitude or, indeed, even a philosophy, which focuses more on thinking, logic and the development of analytical skills than on the physical processes of using a compass or setting a map.

Problem-solving in navigation

Good navigation, knowing exactly where you are the majority (if not all) of the time, takes many years to acquire. In our everyday lives we are not used to the concept of being lost. We tend to spend most of our time in familiar surroundings, with our own landmarks and reference points. When we stray away from home, it is usually on a bus or train when the route itself provides a checking system for our direction, or in the car when the speed of travel and the efficiency of modern-day road signs ensure that we are only really ever temporarily lost. On foot, in mountainous terrain, however, it is a different story. We travel more slowly, with considerable physical effort, especially if carrying an expedition rucksack and, therefore, if we have walked down a parallel, but wrong, valley to the one we intended to use to reach our destination, we have the thankless task of crossing over a ridge, or retracing our steps, with all the physical discomfort and energy-sapping time which this entails.

If we encourage young people to adopt a problem-solving approach to navigation, they will, at every point where a decision as to the intended direction has to be taken, do two important things. First, they will go through the hard skill process of navigating and route-finding using the map and compass; secondly, they will also consider all other options available to them, in detail, until they have confirmed that the route selected is the correct one. This process of group negotiation may take a little longer in time, but this is nothing compared with the effort of later correcting a wrong decision. Such techniques can be especially helpful when encountering bad weather. If the group can see conditions approaching which will result in poor visibility – a cloud front, low cloud cover, mist or whatever – they should take the opportunity, every few minutes, of identifying their exact position and setting compass bearings for the next few stages of their route. This way, they will not be suddenly and unexpectedly left without any visual reference points; simply by taking a bearing on a spot feature while it is still visible, rather than trying to work solely from the oriented map and hoping that they are correct.

This is also a wise practice to follow in the evening. Once the campsite for the night has been reached, tents set up and some members of the group have begun cooking supper, another couple of members should look at the next day's route, double check the bearings with the features which they can see while it is still daylight, and even set the bearing on a compass which will be left untouched until morning. In this way, if there is a thick mist when they get up in the morning, the group will be setting off with preprepared information, and a feeling of confidence, rather than starting the day feeling lost or misguided.

Weighing up all the options

We can apply exactly the same process of problem-solving by considering all the possible options open to us if we should ever become lost (or perhaps one should say 'navigationally challenged' nowadays?). 'On Being Lost' is the title of a chapter in *Land Navigation: Routefinding with Map and Compass* (Keay, 1989), which takes a very logical, systematic and problem-based approach to navigation. Keay includes in the chapter a superb piece of joined-up thinking in the form of a question and action chart which should, I feel, be standard issue to every group of young people setting off on a foot expedition. This chart, shown in Figure 6.1, sets out the systematic process to be followed to return the group to their intended route. It is, like all good ideas, simplicity itself. For example, if the reason you are lost is merely that you are at a different place to that which you originally intended, and you can accurately identify the new point at which you have arrived, you are not lost; you are just not where you wanted to be. The answer, therefore, is to either plan a new route to the original destination or, if you are still on-route, just make your way to where you wanted to be.

The logical process of the question and action chart is that the end result, eventually, is always being able to proceed to the original, intended destination, even if several intermediary stages are passed through along the way. This shows the young person that there is a practical and logical way of proceeding if lost, rather than to assume that there is no way out of the problem.

STOP – NOTE TIME
SET MAP USING COMPASS – COMPARE MAP AND COUNTRY

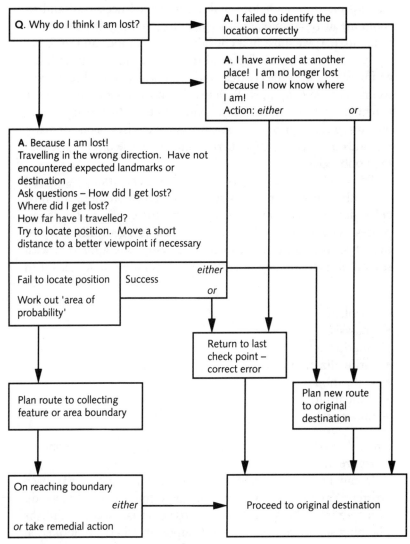

Figure 6.1 On being lost: question and action chart
Source: Keay (1989)

The design process

In order to promote in our young people this ability to analyse all possible options before making informed decisions, and to spontaneously adopt the approach suggested by the flowchart in Figure 6.1, we must first consider what methods and tools we can use to teach them. We need to look outside the traditional confines of our subject area and find which interdisciplinary techniques we can apply. Perhaps the most obvious vehicle for teaching problem-solving as a skill, rather than through time-tabled subjects which use problem-based exercises as one of many methods of teaching their curriculum, is the use of design-based methodologies.

The teaching of design as a subject is, very often, associated with other curriculum areas such as graphic communication or craft, design and technology. However, the concept of a design process is common to all of these areas and it is generally accepted that this process can be defined as a systematic approach with several distinct and key stages. These stages are usually identified as:

- problem
- analysis
- solution
- rationalization
- realization
- evaluation
- modification

An outline of a common variation of the design process is shown in Figure 6.2.

It can be seen, therefore, that once this process has been written down it can have an immediate impact on our expedition training. The most obvious cross-over is, of course, to the planning sequence described in Chapter 4, where we looked at the concept of problem-solving in planning. The design process, as a way of considering all possible alternatives before selecting

PROBLEM	What are we going to design?
ANALYSIS	Think about it. Find reference material (i.e. examples from books or magazines). Put all thoughts and ideas on paper using sketches and notes.
SOLUTION	Chose the best idea. Why is this the most suitable design? What size will it be? Are the proportions correct and aesthetically pleasing?
RATIONALIZATION	How long will it take to produce? What specialist equipment will be needed to make it? What materials will be needed? How must will it cost to make? Will you need to learn any new skills and techniques?
REALIZATION	Make it!
EVALUATION	Is it the same as the original design? Will it do the job for which it was designed? What have you learnt? Could the design be improved?
MODIFICATION	What changes are necessary, and why? What improvements need to be made?

Figure 6.2 The design process

a final solution, could easily be applied to any aspect of our venture from the choice of destination to the transport. The process can, however, be beneficially used with the participants to encourage them to consider all implications of their decision-making, rather than rely on a recommendation from the leaders. It could, for example, be adapted to look at many aspects of an individual's venture; what equipment to carry, what food to eat or, even, at seperate items of equipment.

A design-based approach to selecting equipment

All too often, young people will be advised, or even told, what equipment they require. Rather than being prescriptive, as in the 'you'll need a pair of boots like these' approach, we can introduce necessary items of equipment from a different perspective. We can set the design parameters, for each problem to be solved, as individual, practical, exercises:

- You will be walking for two days, covering at least 16 kilometres each day.
- You will be walking across open moorland, with the occasional rocky outcrop.
- You are carrying rucksacks containing all necessary camping equipment and food.
- The weather is likely to be cold and wet.

Question: What footwear do you think would be most appropriate?

Participants can then simply list down the desired and required performance of their footwear and then, alongside it, suggest a feature that would provide this performance. Such a system can be used for any item of equipment, and it may even be possible for blank forms, such as that in Figure 6.3, to be produced so that the selection of all items of equipment becomes a decision-making process.

Such forms can, initially, be completed by each individual participant, and then broadened into a group discussion. A

ITEM OF EQUIPMENT	
DESIRED PERFORMANCE	REQUIRED FEATURE

Figure 6.3 Example equipment form

completed example of the form is shown in Figure 6.4. Some desired performance criteria will have been selected by many of the group while some criteria will have been selected by only a few. Each point could be discussed by the group as a whole until

WALKING BOOTS	
DESIRED PERFORMANCE	**REQUIRED FEATURE**
Non-slip on mud and rocks.	Solid, rubber 'Commando' type sole.
Ankle support when carrying weight.	Solid leather, lacing up over ankle length.
Rigid while walking on rocks.	Three-quarter length shank.
Comfort – no blisters.	Padded, seam and crease free, lining.
Waterproof (or waterproofable).	Sewn-in tongue, few external seams.
Minimum shock to the joints.	'Rebound' type insole.
Easily laced and unlaced.	Hooks and external eyelets. Strong laces.

Figure 6.4 Example of a completed equipment form

a mastersheet for that particular item of equipment has been produced, for use by that particular group at that particular time, as the requirements of each group and every experience are likely to vary and it would be wrong simply to hand each successive group a stock list if we are trying to encourage problem-solving. Examples of various different footwear could then be displayed by the leader and the merits and faults of each discussed. It would be an interesting exercise to see if commercially available equipment met all of the design parameters set by the group and whether different examples of the same items of equipment (such as various brands and makes of boots) in differing price bands could be compared against each other to find a 'best buy in group'.

As it is unlikely that our young people will, initially, be using their boots to trek in the high mountain regions of the world, the group can discuss what are the core features necessary in boots required to undertake the activities which they have selected or with which they are involved, and what desired features may be able to be sacrificed for the sake of economy. Each participant will then have an informed opinion as to the performance they require from their footwear and, because of this process, hopefully understand why boots are important, rather than buying boots simply because they are on the kit list issued by the leader.

A design-based approach to expedition rations

What food to take is a decision most, if not all, ventures have to consider a some stage; whether this be a simple mountain day-walk, when a flask, packed lunch and a pocket full of chocolate bars will often suffice, or a major expedition where the composition, storage and carrying of food are all important considerations. Dr Mike Stroud and Sir Ranulph Fiennes calculated that they were expending an average of 6,500 kilocalories a day hauling their sledges across the Antarctic on skis, and that, on some days, this could rise to 10,000 kcal. This, for them, was vital information as food not only provides the body with energy and power to keep on the move but, in polar regions, because of the cold, calories can be burned up by the body at a rate faster than they can be replaced. David Mitchell and Stephen Martin, on the Transpolar Drift Stream Expedition, found it extremely difficult to get much more than 6,000 kcal out of the one-kilogram-per-day rations which their sledge weights allowed them to carry. They settled, therefore, on a high-fat diet and their daily food intake does not sound too appetizing: tea and a mush of caramel and banana cereal with dried milk, suet and peanut butter, followed by Horlicks for breakfast; a litre of fortified soup, chocolate with hazelnuts, salami and a munch bar of their own recipe (suet, nuts and honey) during the day while they were towing their sledges and, for an evening meal, dehydrated meat, mash and suet followed by Horlicks (see Radford, 1994).

Because of the extremes of temperature, Arctic and Antarctic expeditions have always planned their rations carefully. Shackleton's expedition in 1914 carried half-pound blocks of their own invention, composed of lard, oatmeal, beef protein, vegetable protein, salt and sugar which had to be boiled up with snow. When things got tough the expedition members would thicken it with seal blubber or bits of penguin meat and then tip in cocoa or marmalade or anything else that remained in their food store.

Although it is very unlikely that the sort of expeditions and ventures with which we will be involved with our young people will require such rarefied diets, these examples illustrate, nevertheless, how important it is to give due consideration to the food we need to consume during a physically demanding venture. Rather than just issuing a sealed ration pack from the stores or purchasing a prepared dehydrated meal from an outdoor shop, we can encourage participants to adopt a problem-solving approach to their food which will help them to understand their body's requirements for energy while on the expedition and also the types of food that will sustain them over the venture, as well as being convenient to carry and cook and appetizing to eat.

The ability to think is promoted through this process and issues can be thought through in advance which may, in time, greatly enhance the outcome of the venture itself. A trail of desired outcomes against requirements can be produced:

Desired outcome: A hot evening meal.
Requirements: Food, stove, fuel, matches.

If a hot evening meal is desired, all of the requirements have to be in place and operational. If any one of the four items malfunctions or is lost, a hot meal cannot be provided. Some, such as the matches, can be backed up with spares, but the fuel is often too heavy to have more than a slight additional margin in reserve and even that extra is often carried in the same bottle. If, therefore, we are carrying dehydrated food, which requires rehydrating and heating before it is edible, we have a number of vital requirements on which our meal depends. It may be that, with some prior thought, we decide to carry food which, although possibly a little heavier, could be eaten cold in an emergency. All these factors can be considered and weighed up in advance and, a vital part of the design process, tested *before* the actual venture. In this way many things can be accomplished at home and in comfort before all the other demands of the venture are upon us. The time food takes to cook can be accurately checked and the amount of fuel required to cook it can be worked out. Spices or flavourings can be added to bland meals. Portions can be worked out exactly. Complementary menus, in terms of a balanced intake of fats and carbohydrates, can be devised and, very importantly, food that we enjoy eating and can cook easily can be prepared for the venture itself. A balanced diet for an expedition can be designed, evaluated, modified and revised in exactly the same way as any item of equipment. Figure 6.5 shows a design-based approach to expedition rations.

In order for this approach to work, we need to allow our young people to look at all the decisions they have to make throughout their involvement in Outdoor Education as problems to be solved. This process can be a continual loop and, if practised at home prior to the venture, they will be able to implement any modifications arising from the evaluation of their decision, rather than sitting in a cold and wet tent, having prepared a particular meal for the first time, wishing that the menu had been tested beforehand.

PROBLEM	What are we going to eat on our expedition?
ANALYSIS	Find example menus from mountaineering textbooks. What do we eat normally at home, would this be suitable? Visit supermarkets on a fact-finding mission to see what is available. How much energy (calories) will we use up on our expedition? Do any members of the group have special dietary requirements?
SOLUTION	Select what we think is our most suitable menu. Is there sufficient variety? Are the foods we have selected freely available? Does the menu provide sufficient energy? Will our diet be properly balanced?
RATIONALIZATION	How much does all our food weigh, can we carry it? How much will it cost to buy? Will it keep, or perish? How will we pack it? Can it be cooked on the stoves we will be using on the expedition? Can it be eaten cold, if we run out of fuel, or in an emergency?
REALIZATION	Try the menu out, at home, in a dummy run.
EVALUATION	Did you enjoy the food? Was it easy to cook? Did it create much waste; were the pans hard to clean? What did it taste like cold?
MODIFICATION	Can we improve the menu? Would a little seasoning or sauce make it tastier? What would we change and why?
FINAL SOLUTION	Being well fed throughout the expedition.

Figure 6.5 A design-based approach to expedition rations

Learning to expect the unexpected

It may help to devise a series of factors, in the form of questions which need to be resolved, to provide the best solution. Figure 6.6 shows some of the many questions which may be considered. There are, of course, many more.

CARRYING	How much does the food weigh? How much space will it take up? How bulky is it (i.e., large but light)? How fragile is it (i.e., eggs)? What containers does it need? Can we measure out exact amounts beforehand? Can it 'go off' or melt when carrying?
COOKING	Does it need water (i.e., dehydrated)? How long does it take to cook? Is it easy to prepare and cook? What utensils does it require when cooking? What attention does it require when cooking?
EATING	Is it perishable, or can we keep any leftovers? What nutritional value does it have? What does it taste like? Could it be eaten cold in an emergency? Can it be precooked at home and warmed up on expedition?
CLEANING	What waste does it leave (i.e., tins, fat, etc.)? What cleaning of pans is required? Can it be cooked in its own containers? Is waste biodegradable?
COST/GENERAL	Where can we buy it? Is it expensive? What quantities does it come in? If any is left, will it keep until the next expedition? Is it cheap enough to experiment with beforehand?

Figure 6.6 Factors for consideration

In the same way as we used the Doidge, Bone and Hardwick (1996) illustration of the problem-solving process in Chapter 4 (see Figure 4.6) we can lay out this problem-solving approach to expedition rations in diagrammatic form, as illustrated in Figure 6.7, to show that we are concerned with a process, rather than a list. This illustration refines our 'design' to show that we could be considering solutions for either an individual member or for the group as a whole. There are, of course, instances where the decision as to what equipment to take will, by necessity, be a group one; the type of tent being a good example. However, other items of equipment will be more a matter of individual preference and the final choice of equipment such as a sleeping bag may be influenced by specific factors unique to each member of the group: whether they are allergic to feathers or certain materials, how much they feel the cold, their physical size and strength, how much weight they are prepared to carry and even their available budget. Many personal factors will determine each individual's selection.

Refining existing equipment

De Bono says that there are three types of problem. He maintains that the first type requires, for its solution, more information or better techniques for handling information. Solutions to the second type of problem require no new information, but a rearrangement of information already available. The third type of problem is what de Bono calls the problem of no problem:

> One is blocked by the adequacy of the present arrangement from moving to a much better one. There is no point at which one can focus one's efforts to reach the better arrangement because one is not even aware that there is a better arrangement. The problem is to realise that there is a problem – to realise that things can be improved and to define this realisation as a problem. (De Bono, 1977, p. 53)

This is, perhaps, where Outdoor Education has so much to contribute; solving a problem which does not, as yet, exist. At a

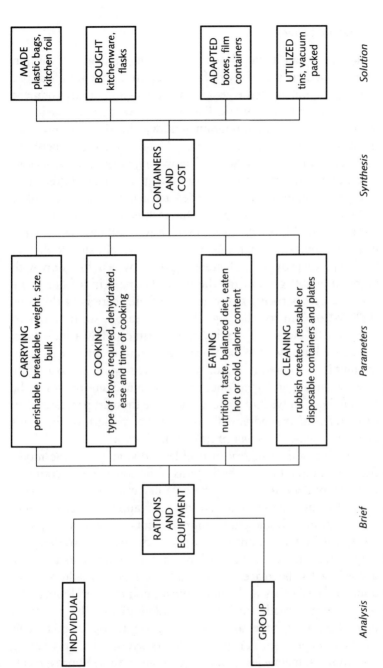

Figure 6.7 A problem-solving approach to expedition rations

| Analysis | Brief | Parameters | Synthesis | Solution |

basic level it can be the close scrutiny of equipment to ascertain when, or where, it is likely to fail or require subtle modification. This can be linked to the geographical situation or environment in which we intend to work. For example, we may have selected to use a lightweight mountain tent which, after careful consideration, we adjudge to provide a suitable balance between size, strength and pack weight. However, we need to consider whether all aspects of the tent suit our individual requirements. The manufacturer may, in order to achieve lightness, have included aluminium tent pegs. Our task is to consider whether these are suitable for the terrain which we shall be experiencing. It may be that, although our intended overnight stop looks, on the map, to provide a sheltered spot in which to camp with potentially soft ground for the pegs, the majority of our route takes us across rocky, stony ground where there is likely to be shallow top soil for the pegs. For this reason, we may opt to carry a little increased weight, in the form of a few 4-inch nails, which we know we will be able to drive into rocky soil securing the tent if we are required, for whatever reason, to camp at a site other than our intended one, or our planned site proves to be less idyllic than we had hoped. The same thought processes can, of course, be applied equally well to the strength of the tent's poles or any other aspect of its overall design.

Also into this category of problem-solving comes the modification of equipment. Whether this is the considered scrutiny of new equipment to detect where faults may occur, or where improvements could be made, or the renovation of older gear with the addition of home-made improvements; even at a simplistic level, it is better to reinforce seams or fixtures before they give way. There are even adaptations that we may wish to make according to the places to be visited on our expedition. The addition of sewn-in, and zipped, mosquito net inner doors to the tent (possibly made out of net curtaining) may be a distinct advantage if we are anticipating encountering insects! This process encourages participants to look critically at what is, effectively, someone else's design. Of course, these improvements to designs do not actually have to be carried out, it is the process of encouraging young people to look at equipment critically which is important, as it allows them to understand the purpose for which the item was designed and provides them with a greater insight into the activities which they will be undertaking. A visit to an outdoor equipment suppliers, or a browse through an equipment catalogue, could lead to discussion on how items of commercially available equipment can be improved upon.

Processes, not just items of equipment

Tent pitching

It has always fascinated me how leaders decide when to teach their participants how to put up tents. We normally chose a sunny Sunday afternoon, or a pleasant dry evening, on the flat and even surface of the school's playing fields or a piece of land outside the youth club. But when do the young people actually put up their tents? Usually at the end of a hard day's walk, when they are tired and possibly irritable, often in the rain and wind, sometimes in the dark, on a bleak and exposed uneven piece of wet scrubland with the added handicap of an apparent substrata of rocks half an inch below the surface. If we are serious about promoting a problem-solving approach, we should chose the most unpleasant, windy and rain-lashed evening to teach them how to put up the tents. It is amazing how the speed of tent pitching improves in direct proportion to the inclemency of the weather.

Let them consider the problems, before they arise for real, in a situation which is safe and controlled and in which they can have the luxury of time to consider, test, evaluate and improve various options. Could they, for example, erect a tent on the tarmac surface of a car park, or inside a classroom? This may lead them to consider methods other than tent pegs for pinning the tent to the ground. Weights, rocks, or tied to trees and fences, they can attempt as many solutions as they can devise. This has

175

two significant advantages: first, it allows them to appreciate the function of even simple pieces of equipment such as the tent peg and how all the little items add up to ensure the success of their plans; secondly, by problem-solving imaginary scenarios in the safety of a classroom, the group is less likely to be thrown into panic if a real problem besets them while on the venture.

The publication *In Search of Adventure* recognizes this increased adoption of a problem-solving approach within Outdoor Education:

> Essentially, the participant is required to discover rather than being provided with the answer. Even the task of working out for themselves how to erect their tent may have far greater learning potential for a group than simply copying a method demonstrated by an instructor. (Hunt, 1989, p. 164)

As the expression goes, practice makes perfect, and such a problem-solving approach can be extended, through the use of tasks becoming gradually more difficult, until the group are so at ease with the use of their equipment that they could even put up the tent while blindfolded with one seeing person giving instructions from a distance or even as a group with, quite literally, one arm tied behind their backs.

This approach can be taken with the young people out into the countryside; the only limit is their imagination. It would not be an exaggeration to say that participants could be encouraged to problem-solve, or design, every aspect of their venture. A campsite, for example, can be designed in exactly the same way as a landscape painter designs a composition; where will the light come from, where will the wind come from, which part of the site will be in shade. All these are vital parts of putting up a tent in a comfortable situation, yet they are often taught from the basis of a bland statement of fact, such as 'always pitch the rear of the tent facing into the wind', rather than from an analytical perspective of discovering, from observing trees or other surrounding features, or analysing, from a hand-held 'wind sock' or a small piece of cloth fixed to the end of a tent peg or stick, which direction the wind is blowing in.

Rucksack packing

Similarly, we should encourage participants to consider when they think they will actually need to use the torch which we insist they carry with them. The obvious answer is in the dark. So, if we blindfold them and get them to practice finding their torch in their well-packed rucksacks, they will be able to find it in the real situation when there is only limited visibility. Not only that, but the young people will realize why we encourage them to pack the torch in a place which is readily accessible, they will have understood, rather than repeating a process parrot fashion. The same applies for the first aid kit. It is easy to slowly find and display the contents if we are just checking what gear we have with us before the commencement of our venture, but what if we need to use our first aid kit for real? The panic and adrenaline rush of an incident – no matter how small or, after the event, relatively insignificant – makes our actions unreliable. To overcome this 'panic factor' services such as the Fire Brigade will practice using equipment, under carefully controlled conditions, in dummy houses and rooms filled with dense smoke. They will repeat certain techniques until they become automatic and instinctive, so that when the manoeuvre is deployed in real-life situations, the fireman does not have to think about every little nuance of the process, he just does it.

I am not suggesting that we go to these lengths in training young people for expeditions, but I do feel that we could be more creative in our methodology. Instead of giving a lecture on why it is important to pack certain items of equipment in easily accessible parts of the rucksack, so that they can be retrieved in moments of crisis, get young people to practise running up to their rucksack, finding the first aid kit, and getting out a wound dressing. We, as trainers, could use such techniques, possibly as impromptu relay races (when the participants do not know what item of kit they will each be required, in turn, to produce) until the action of finding certain pieces of equipment becomes second nature.

177

What equipment to take?

The selection of equipment for the expedition provides an ideal focus for the exercising of a problem-solving approach to outdoor activities. We are immediately in a dilemma; we must take sufficient gear to be safe, comfortable and self-sufficient over the duration of the venture, but we must not take so much that our pack weights end up so heavy as to have exactly the opposite results: uncomfortable, overloaded and dangerous. The choice of equipment, not only the selection of light-weight variations of necessary equipment, but whether we need that particular item of gear at all, becomes a mind-taxing process. If we are wrong and take too much kit, we will end up carrying unnecessary weight around for the duration of the venture with the consequences suggested above. If we take too little, and do not have that vital bit of equipment when we need it, the resulting lack of comfort and erosion of our safety margins will be the same.

This makes the progressive and developmental nature of well-planned Outdoor Education very pertinent. It is through training days and practice journeys that young people, and their more experienced leaders alike, can experiment with load carrying, try out different combinations of gear, field test certain items of equipment and generally modify their rucksacks to contain the combination of equipment which provides for us (and us alone as we all have differing carrying abilities and 'comfort zones' of how much hardship we can tolerate) the best compromise, and it will be a compromise, as our aim is to provide the maximum of comfort and safety with the minimum of excess weight.

There is, however, another element in this formula of what gear to take, and that is for which items of equipment you will need a spare. Examples such as a torch bulb are obvious, as the torch itself (and the weight of the batteries) would not be worth carrying if the all important, and lightweight, bulb failed to work. But should we, for example, also carry spare batteries?

All too often, young people are presented with an equipment list which lists items such as: Torch (and spare bulb and batteries). It is very easy for leaders to take the short cut of stipulating equipment to avoid the potential danger of participants being without a vital piece of gear. It is, after all, extremely difficult to undertake any form of night navigation or cooking in the dark if you do not have a means of illuminating your map and compass or stove.

But why not take a slightly different view of the same problem of what 'spares' to take. We can divide our gear up into two categories: first, those items which we feel are most likely to get lost, broken or wear out; second, those items which, if they were to be mislaid, broken or worn out, would have a detrimental effect on the venture. Through this process, we may find that some items will appear in both categories, for example, the compass is very easy to put down at a rest stop only to leave it behind, and so is easy to lose. Such a loss could also have a far-reaching effect on the group's success, as a party without a compass, attempting to navigate in poor visibility, will be at an extreme disadvantage. We must ensure, therefore, that the group themselves decide that, if they do not have the optimum of one compass each, they have at least two, if not three, compasses among them.

Once participants have made their own two lists (three, if we count the overlaps) and possibly even converted the written lists into Venn diagrams, we can use this as a focus for discussion until the group reach an agreement as to exactly what gear to carry. Not only will they have understood the rationale behind the selection of gear, but they will also know the relative importance of each item they have with them and know that they are carrying it for a purpose rather than simply because they were told to do so. Through this process, the group may decide to double up on some items thus solving in advance, any potential future problem. The notion of problem-solving should not just be about finding solutions to problems which have happened but, as de Bono suggests, pre-empting any future problem, seeing the unforseen or expecting the unexpected!

First aid

The selection of first aid equipment is a classic example where participants are occasionally directed into a solution rather than allowed to find one for themselves. Often, groups are presented with a sealed first aid kit from the central stores which will probably remain sealed until it is returned at the end of the expedition. The young people will, hopefully, know what is in the kit as they should at least be provided with a list, but as they have not put the kit together, do they really understand why each item is included and why certain items have been excluded? If this is the case, another valuable learning situation has been lost. Outdoor Education should, after all, be as much about education, in its widest sense, as it is about the outdoors.

The first element in this process is for the young people to consider what accidents are likely to befall them during the venture for which they would have the necessary equipment to provide effective first aid. In this respect they are beginning a process which can, eventually, be extended into the risk assessments described in Chapter 3. Experience has taught us that the overwhelming proportion of first aid on expeditions will be required for blisters, minor cuts and small burns; in that order. At least one member of the group will, in all probability, experience blisters during a foot expedition and their first aid kit should, therefore, reflect this. It seems logical to take equipment to deal with only what is likely to happen, rather than, for example, carrying around complex apparatus to deal with snake bites if your venture is taking place in the UK. This makes the selection of equipment one of the best examples in Outdoor Education for putting into practice a design-based, problem-solving approach. We traditionally look at design as being something which involves the production of tangible objects: cars, clothes, furniture and the like. However, the accepted problem-solving process of designing–making–evaluating can, just as easily relate to a function by becoming designing–doing–evaluating and such functions can equally be selecting equipment as an individual or a practical teamwork exercise.

Problem-solving or problem-setting?

Many residential courses include a session of what are often called problem-solving or teamwork exercises. I must state, from the outset, that I feel that this is totally valid if it is a session which is used in a transitory sense in that it is taking the participants from one mode of operation to another. It is important that, if we encourage groups of young people to explore the concept of problem-solving (and, of course, through this, the notion of working together as a team) in what is, all too often, an artificial situation with artificial problems, we must allow them to subsequently translate this into real problems in a real environment. There is often a temptation for young people to sense that the problem-solving exercise is a practical conundrum set by the leaders to which there is a definite answer (which the leaders, of course, know) and which it is the group's job, to discover. They need to be convinced that the problem is open-ended and that the solution at which they arrive may work just as well as a totally different solution arrived at by another group.

We have to be careful not to fall into what I have termed the 'problem-setting trap'. This is where there is an empty afternoon on the residential course or venture and we attempt to fill it usefully by making participants mess around with some rope, planks and a few old oil drums. I have certainly heard delegates (admittedly adults) in such sessions say, during the debrief, 'we knew the solution immediately, but we thought that what you wanted was for us to discuss it and try out various options before arriving at the solution; so that's what we did'. It is important, therefore, for the participants to appreciate that it is the skill of problem-solving which such sessions are attempting to foster, rather that setting a practical test, or a trick question, for them to solve as quickly as they can. These sessions must lead into the group taking their new-found skills into real-life situations where they are required to problem-solve as a team so that they can recognize and appreciate the transferability of the problem-solving approach they are developing.

181

In this respect, like so much else in Outdoor Education, the reflective stage, or the debrief/review session is the key to progress. The whole team reflecting on the total performance, as well as each individual assessing both their own contribution and the input of others, is a true example of the 360-degree feedback discussed in Chapter 4. This can often place a heavy burden on the leader, or facilitator, of the activity, as the group will want suggestions as to what went wrong and when, or praise on elements when they all pulled together as a cohesive unit. This requires skilful handling by the facilitator who generally assumes the role of passive observer during the exercises themselves, giving no hints as to progress or possible solutions, and then acts, if necessary, as a chairman or prompt during the review. In this respect, the increasing use of video cameras to provide instant, and indisputable, feedback can be very beneficial even if only to illustrate the participation – or lack of it – by certain members of the group at certain times.

Many excellent publications and a considerable amount of resource material is now available on problem-solving exercises and, with a little imagination, they can be a creative and stimulating addition to our outdoor training programmes. The big advantage, of course, is that such exercises can be set up almost anywhere and can, therefore, be used as a entertaining session during a break in an evening's training or even, with a small amount of easily transported equipment, be set up to relieve the monotony of a long journey on the way to a wild country area for a practice expedition or a residential trip.

Conclusion

Successful problem-solving is embodied in an approach or an attitude which, if promoted in young people through participation in Outdoor Education, will have benefits across all aspects of their lives, especially within their school or college, where an enquiring mind and an ability to look at problems rationally and logically is an advantage in all subjects, and later in their working careers where employers place much value on such qualities. The techniques of the design-based approach, suggested above, must be recognized, therefore, as a core skill rather than being compartmentalized as something the young people do only while on expeditions or engaged in the outdoor activity.

7 All stressed up and nowhere to go: The post-experience implications of adventurous activities

Experience is never limited, and it is never complete;
it is an immense sensibility, a kind of huge spider-web
of the finest silken threads suspended in the chamber of
    consciousness,
and catching every air-borne particle in its tissue.
Henry James, Prefaces (1909)

Post-holiday blues

'Why so many holidays end in dark despair' was the subheading for an article entitled 'The back-to-work blues' in the *Mail on Sunday* newspaper of 4 September 1994. The item detailed the sense of disillusionment, despair, fatigue and depression which American psychiatrist Dr Ross Goldstein (1994) suggests accompany the sinking feeling which we all often feel on returning to work after a holiday when 'you come back feeling healthy and relaxed, only for your high spirits to fade as quickly as your tan'. Dr Goldstein reports that around 50 per cent of his clients who consult him for career issues do so immediately after a vacation and contends that he has identified a specific clinical psychological condition, which he terms 're-entry syndrome', in which adults, while on holiday and divorced from the ties of the workplace, gain objectivity and set about planning what they will do on their return to work. Some go as far as planning a career move, others set themselves targets such as starting a fitness programme or attending an evening class but, as they return from holiday and find themselves slipping back into their old lives and routines, they feel a terrible sense of devastation and failure.

This phenomenon is very similar to a condition identified in Britain by Professor Cary Cooper (1992), Organizational Psychologist at the Institute of Science and Technology at the University of Manchester (UMIST) who calls his version 'post-holiday stress'. Professor Cooper, in an article in the *Evening Standard* (Gruner, 1992), takes the view that modern working life has become so stressful that there is a very stark dividing line between leisure and work, and that people use holidays as a mechanism for dealing with the stress they build up in the course of a year. However, they are generally so worn out by the summer that the annual holiday can never meet up to such heavy expectations. Like Dr Goldstein, Professor Cooper acknowledges that the considerable pressures of life make the holiday a significant event and feels that the idea that people need an extra week off, to recover from the holiday, before easing themselves back into work mode, is a serious suggestion. Professor Cooper contends that learning to relax is an art form and that, with the modern pace of life, it can take about thirteen days to totally relax; at which stage the conventional two-week holiday is over and the stress of work is, once again, upon us.

Redundancy in the workplace and 'survivor syndrome'

The idea of there being a psychological response in the aftermath of a major event in someone's life is not new although there has, in recent years, been a steady growth in the identification, and naming, of specific clinical conditions. The world-wide recession during the early 1990s saw considerable change in the workplace. Many companies undertook programmes of restructuring in attempts to remain competitive in their sector of the market and this was often accompanied by right-sizing (or down-sizing, depending on how cynical ones viewpoint is) being the removal of large numbers of employees through voluntary or compulsory redundancy in order to make efficiency gains in the company's output compared to its staffing levels. This climate, quite naturally, brought its own unique stresses to working life; the threat of possible redundancy may stimulate, rather than motivate, employees into working harder in the short term, but, in the long term, it does not generally do much for a worker's loyalty, job satisfaction or their industrial relations with the employer.

Studies into the psychological effects of the free market culture have been well recorded elsewhere. What is of interest in the context of this chapter, however, is a condition named 'survivor syndrome' identified by a survey undertaken in the autumn of 1994 by Working Transitions and Cranfield's Human Resource Research Centre (quoted in Doherty and Horsted, 1995). The survey, which collated the opinions of 170 personnel and human resources specialists in 131 financial services institutions employing over 500,000 staff throughout the UK, identified the reactions of decreased motivation, a lowering of morale and reduced loyalty to the company coupled with increased stress levels and scepticism often exhibited by remaining employees following redundancies in their organizations. When large-scale changes in the workforce are made, employees often stated that they experienced some of the disbelief and sense of loss which follows a bereavement. For those remaining in employment with the company, the so-called survivors, there was, in addition to a sense of loss, a feeling of guilt about having a job when ex-colleagues now did not. It is interesting to note that while 79 per cent of the respondents to the survey had programmes in place to help employees who were being made redundant, structured policies to help those remaining were very much less evident, with very little emphasis on counselling the survivors on personal change or careers. This may be one reason why a recent survey by the Policy Studies Institute found that 67 per cent of professional and managerial staff felt work stress had increased in the last five years and why many companies are turning to workplace counsellors to help employees cope with the often drastic changes taking place within organizations (Maxwell Magnus, 1995). John Whapham (1995), deputy chair of the Association for Counselling at Work, has been quoted as saying:

A few years ago, going to a counsellor would be seen as a loss of face, especially in macho cultures like the police force, but now you'll find even chief superintendents writing about their experience of it in the staff magazine. It's become a great deal more acceptable.

This picture is also seen in other sectors of the workforce and professions when examples such as a junior doctor who gave up his job because of depression and was given £5,600 damages by his previous employer, or a social worker who received compensation after suffering a second nervous breakdown caused by an unbearable workload, are reported almost on a daily basis in the press.

Natural disasters and caring for the carers

We have looked at the effects suffered by people surviving a trauma in their working life, whether through the stress of changed conditions or redundancy, although – personally – I prefer the word 'remainers' to signify those who remain in employment after large-scale changes in personnel, so that the classification of survivor can be used when, in the true sense of the word, someone has lived through or witnessed an event which has threatened their physical integrity – in other words a situation where they may well have lost their life or which has claimed the lives of others.

We read every day in the newspapers of large-scale natural disasters: floods, famine, earthquake. Such stories remain in the headlines for perhaps a week before being largely forgotten by the rest of the world. Natural disasters have a tremendous physical impact on the area in which they occur which can often take many years to rebuild. On a human scale, they also have a far-reaching emotional effect on those who lose family or friends, those who lose their homes or belongings, those who witness the terror at first hand or for those volunteers or members of the emergency services who, very often, put themselves in danger to assist in the control of the disaster.

Into this category must also come people who have survived traumatic events such as the King's Cross Station fire or the Hillsborough football stadium tragedy. Those victims who were suddenly caught up in events, as well as the police, ambulance and fire service personnel who attended the scene many of whom have suffered the effects of a condition which has come to be termed 'post-traumatic stress'. Of particular interest to this work, which is focused on the activities of young adults, is the number of teenage St John Ambulance cadets on duty at the Hillsborough stadium, as part of the normal first aid cover, who must have been severely traumatized by witnessing the deaths of fans crushed to death as the cadets fought to save them through the fences against which the victims were trapped by the sheer human weight of people pressing down, in panic, above them.

Although the incidents quoted are of a large scale, and have the resultant world-wide media interest, we must not forget those who, in their everyday life, are suddenly involved in a shocking and unexpected event: trauma victims involved in car crashes, assaults, rapes and hostage situations as well as bystanders in working life, such as railway employees who subsequently need counselling to help them deal with the post-traumatic stress caused by witnessing accidents on level crossings or suicides on railway lines.

Shell-shock, combat fatigue and post-traumatic stress disorder

The notion of people experiencing ongoing symptoms of stress following close involvement in life threatening situations is especially pertinent for psychiatrists working with ex-servicemen. The concept of shell-shock was introduced during the First World War, although the condition was a long way from being recognized as a psychological post-trauma disorder; some soldiers suffering from severe shell-shock were court-martialled, and subsequently executed by firing squad, for such 'crimes' as refusing to return to the trenches, sleeping at their post, disobedience, throwing away their arms or, as one verdict of a court martial stated 'misbehaving before the enemy in such a manner as to show cowardice' (Landale, 1995). Professional understanding of the condition, the term shell-shock evolving into the more sympathetic description of 'battle fatigue', was considerably refined during the Second World War. It was, however, the collective and individual psychological traumas suffered by returning Vietnam veterans in the USA which highlighted the long-term effects of war experience. Post-traumatic stress disorder (PTSD), diagnosed by American psychiatrists in the 1970s and only officially recognized by the medical establishment after its appearance in America's *Diagnostic and Statistical Manual of Mental Disorders* (1980), describes the persistent psychological distress in Vietnam veterans and has now been very well documented. Closer to home (where the condition is more simply referred to as post-traumatic stress), much work and research has centred around the classic symptoms, such as general anxiety, emotional numbing, unwanted and distressing flashbacks to the incident and re-experiences of the original trauma, over-alertness caused by too much adrenaline and the avoidance of anything – people, places, objects – which could remind them of what happened, suffered by British service personnel returning from the Falklands and Gulf conflicts.

The latest results of a significant survey into the long-term effects of combat, by the American psychiatrist George Valliant, have been published in the May 1995 edition of the *American Journal of Psychiatry* (Lee *et al.*, 1995). The study investigated 268 young men who attended Harvard University between 1939 and 1944 studying them first as students, again on their return to civilian life in 1946 and continuing in great detail ever since. The May 1995 paper reviews the findings 50 years on. In 1946 seventeen of the 268 had displayed two or more of the symptoms of PTSD and only one had been diagnosed as suffering from the full condition. The 1995 results showed that the majority of the sample who had combat-related symptoms in 1946 still had them 50 years later but that the symptoms had not interfered with their

189

lives. Some of the sample had, as could be predicted, suffered from other mental health problems, unrelated to their wartime experiences, over the duration of the study which showed that the PTSD symptoms were associated only with exposure to intense combat and had been observed in all those in the survey who had been injured. In an excellent résumé of the Valliant study, Dr Simon Wessely, writing in *The Times*, concludes that

> what this exceptional study has shown is that psychological reactions to trauma, if they occur, persist. The worse the trauma, the more the symptoms. The normal processes by which we adapt to psychological distress do not seem to happen with such intense experiences. (Wessely, 1995)

Naturally, although memories of the trauma do not disappear, and can still cause distress many years later, those who lived through it can still function normally and many never develop any psychological distress at all.

What has this to do with Outdoor Education?

As has been suggested in earlier chapters, young people have a natural propensity towards excitement and adventure which encompasses the added thrill of encountering risk. As we have seen, an adventurous youth expedition, or residential experience, as part of a programme of Outdoor Education will probably be the most challenging undertaking that a young person has attempted so far in their lives, and may well remain one of the most demanding. It should certainly be a treasured memory which will remain with the young person for a long time to come.

Occasionally we see tangible proof of this, when someone has a significant adventurous experience during their youth and, many years later, still recalls the event vividly, or when such feelings are verbalized or recorded in writing by the young people themselves immediately after the event. As part of my observational research into the emotional after-effects of adventurous outdoor experiences I have encouraged all the young people with whom I have been involved in Outdoor Education to explore and record their feelings on completion of the venture. The following is a quote from an 18-year-old male participant who completed a demanding four-day wilderness foot journey, with a group of four peers, as part of a youth expedition to arctic Norway:

Summary.

I didn't think it was right to have a conclusion. Things like 'Arctic Gold' don't conclude. They're just part of your life from then on. In those four days I learnt things I'll never forget, and shared experiences that will remain memories forever. All of us realised our own capabilities, as we had to improvise, prepare, suffer and use practicality as I, for one, never had before. We also had to learn to work as a team, to tolerate and to compromise. We didn't work together perfectly the whole time. It would be foolish to suggest we couldn't have improved things by doing this or the other. Yet, overall, we achieved something great and, by and large, we did work together, if not perfectly, then at least harmoniously, letting the strengths of each group member come through when they could, and when we weren't so strong, letting others help if needed.

In this log I've tried to accurately record not only what we did, but what we felt. It may seem a little critical, but it was hard not to get irritated at others after several hours tiring walk. And, despite all this, we came through without any major incidents or disagreements, and I can honestly say that I'm proud of the other four I walked with. Nadeem's quick mind and wit; Tejinder's reliability; Peter's endurance and flashes of genius; and especially Kevin, who, despite a difficult couple of days, had the determination not only to carry on, but to also improve by the last day. I would trust my life with them again anytime.

The adventurous experience has obviously been something special to the people involved in the above expedition. As we saw in Chapter 4, they have been through what Abraham Maslow calls a 'peak experience' or an event which, to quote from his

191

book *Toward a Psychology of Being*, 'is felt as a self-validating, self-justifying moment which carries its own intrinsic value with it' (Maslow, 1968, p. 79). We should, surely, if the experience is educationally viable, view young people's participation in outdoor and adventure education in these terms.

It can be argued then, that a shared significant experience in the outdoors, especially if it was perceived as being life threatening, such as may well be the case with rock-climbing or mountaineering in severe conditions, may evoke similar emotions to those observed in the various conditions of re-entry syndrome, post-holiday stress, survivor syndrome or post-traumatic stress described above.

This is not to say that a direct comparison can be made between taking part in a youth expedition and, for example, fighting in the Falklands war. However, if the adventurous Outdoor Education activity should go wrong and there is serious accident or injury, such as in the 1993 Lyme Bay canoeing tragedy, and the rescue services become involved, the participants may experience post-traumatic stress. This has, indeed, been the case with the surviving schoolchildren from Lyme Bay who clung to their overturned canoes in open sea and watched some of their friends drown around them. As reported in *The Times* of 9 December 1994, the trauma had a deep affect on the four girls who survived the incident who subsequently experienced problems with their work and performed disappointingly in their A levels. Their headteacher, June Mowforth, reflected, eighteen months after the event, that 'They are strong in appearance, but I think there is a lot of torment inside. It may take years to come out. But I think they want to get on with things now. They want to look to the future' (Knight, 1994). The survivors, in the true sense of the word, from such, thankfully rare, incidents often need professional support to enable them to come to terms with the events they have experienced, as many symptoms, such as continual anxiety and a feeling of guilt because their friends died and they survived, manifest themselves. The condition of post-traumatic stress, and its treatment, cover this type of extreme outdoor experience and only counselling by trained professionals can enable youngsters to come to terms with the situation.

The vast majority of organized youth adventure, however, passes off without mishap and the need for ongoing counselling of the participants. But this is not to say that the young people do not experience emotional symptoms after the event and need 'bringing down' from the excitement in an informal, although structured, way. We all know, in our private lives, how we discuss significant events with family or friends to help us put things into perspective. Breakdowns of relationships, new jobs, stressful events at work, weddings, births and funerals. We all rely on the informal counselling of those around us to make sense of our lives. I am suggesting, therefore, that all forms of peak experience, both good and bad, need some kind of aftercare, whether formal or informal, to enable the participants to review, evaluate and move on. Those of us involved in Outdoor Education must realize that the effects of the experience on young people can be very long-lasting. In a sense, what would be the point if they weren't?

It must also be remembered that it may simply be the fact that there is always the possibility of things going wrong, the concept of risk as discussed in Chapter 3, which makes Outdoor Education such a valuable tool in the personal and social development of young people. Hopefully, through careful planning and thorough training, the real risk is minimized to an acceptable level, although it is always present. As such, we should, as leaders, recognize that participants may require our help in assimilating the experience during the venture. The thrills of the experience can often provoke intense feelings and we should not be afraid to provide 'emotional first aid' if required.

With this inherent sense of risk, and the emphasis during much of the training on safety procedures, it is not surprising that the final venture or activity can occasionally be viewed with some trepidation. We do not know exactly what the psychological and emotional starting point of all the young people undertaking the activity will be, we merely know that they will all be different. Similarly, we do not always have access to the precise motivating factors behind their voluntary involvement. I certainly know of young people who have participated in any form of residential trip to which they can gain access, not because they were addicted to outdoor activities, but because it was a means of gaining relief from weekends at home where they were regularly beaten by their guardians.

These varied viewpoints can be brought to the fore by the outdoor experience. As we have seen in Chapter 4 when considering the reflective stage of the experience, a high-level, exposed, mountainous ridge walk may be, for one participant, the high point of the venture; they may feel – quite literally – on top of the world and get a real sense of achievement from being there. For another member of the group the same situation at exactly the same moment in time may have totally different connotations; they may be scared stiff and only there because they were carried along by their peers. In these cases their feelings may well override their thinking causing them, possibly, to act out of character. It is important, therefore, that we review such situations as soon as possible after the event, in an atmosphere where all the young people can talk about their emotional experiences of the adventure in an open, constructive and supportive way. I would hope that no sensitive outdoor edu-cationalist would agree with the old theory that hanging young people off exposed rock-faces (often in sheer terror) was some-how character building. This way really does lead to trauma. It is better for young people to try a low-level experience with which they feel comfortable and want to try again, hopefully pushing forward their own personal boundaries, than to force them into an activity which puts them off the outdoors for life.

Burnout

We looked earlier at post-traumatic stress caused by events in the workplace, and it is appropriate to consider again, briefly, parallels between accepted clinical conditions and emotions experienced by young people involved in expeditions. As well as applying to outdoor experiences, the notion of providing review opportunities and counselling is also a prescribed therapy for another form of work-related stress, that of 'burnout'. This is a term describing a condition in which a worker changes from a state of high motivation and efficiency to one of apathy and inefficiency, and possibly even to a state of mild psychological disturbance, through overwork or the pressures of their job. Although it is generally accepted that burnout occurs gradually, in a progressive fashion and, as such, is not strictly relevant to the consideration of post-event trauma in this chapter, there are, nevertheless, striking similarities in symptoms such as feelings of helplessness, hopelessness and disenchantment.

Although there are, of course, similarities with an expedition which may take many months to progress from the concept stage, through the planning stage, to the action stage, it could also be argued that it is often a major event in the workplace which finally acts as the 'trigger' for burnout in an individual and which, thus, gives the false impression that it occurs suddenly. Dr Ludwig Lowenstein, writing in *Education Today*, presents an excellent résumé of research which has been carried out into the prevention and cure of stress in teachers and, in the context of this book on Outdoor Education, it is interesting that, apart from the counselling mention earlier, Dr Lowenstein also cites research into physical factors, such as diet, which have contributed to burnout. In an analysis of diet in teachers working in situations (in this case, special education) which was likely to provoke stress or burnout, it was found that there was; 'a low carbohydrate intake with an over-emphasis on refined carbohydrates, excess protein, but low levels of amino-acids, excess fat, not enough fibre, and insufficient micronutrients' (Lowenstein, 1991, p. 13). It may be, then, that this is the saving grace of expeditions, as, generally, the diet of all participants is carefully controlled to ensure a correctly balanced diet and to provide the energy necessary for the physical demands of the venture. It could also be that the onset of any form of post-event trauma is quickened by a return to the home environment and a change of diet, especially if the young people concerned have an habitual diet of 'junk' food. That, however, is the basis for a different possible piece of research!

Post-residential syndrome

Bearing in mind the varied entry levels, both physical and emotional, of those participating in outdoor activities, we must not forget the great impact that involvement in an adventurous activity can have on young people. They often spend many months planning their venture, with the final expedition or experience being the one thing that binds a collection of individuals together. It becomes an important part of their lives, over an extended time, with weekend practice journeys, the gathering together of equipment, training and planning sessions and, finally, the venture itself. But what then? What happens when the venture is over, the gear packed away and the photos stuck in the album?

Many young people feel a tremendous sense of anti-climax once they have completed the adventurous experience. The event which they have been planning and looking forward to for a long time has been, and gone! The disparate group of young people who formed themselves together into a functioning team to undertake a specific objective, which they have achieved, are suddenly back to being a collection of individuals. Without the regular contact of planning meetings or training sessions, some participants can begin to feel isolated, lonely and depressed. For some young people, such as those who, as we have seen earlier, have varied motivational reasons for being on the venture and differing psychological and emotional needs, involvement in the activity may have, literally, been a lifeline giving them something constant and dependable in their lives. One 22-year-old female participant expressed the feeling of emptiness two weeks after finishing her expedition, by saying: 'It's awful, the worst I've ever felt in my whole life. Everything's so flat. It feels as if my insides have been sucked out.'

Participants reacting in this way are experiencing a condition which, as it encompasses similar symptoms to other post-event conditions outlined at the beginning of this chapter, I have termed 'post-residential syndrome'. In reality it is similar to the post-holiday blues which we experience as adults, but worse. Worse, because of the long-term nature of the planning and training for the adventurous experience, especially in the case of expeditions, which has steadily built up expectations and anticipation, sometimes over a period as long as a year (which is, in many cases, a significant proportion of their young lives), and also because the young people are experiencing such an emotion for possibly the first time. We as adults have learnt through experience that we will feel a little flat after a holiday, a family wedding, starting a new job or other significant event, but the young people have not yet lived through enough peak experiences to have come to terms with the emotions they evoke.

The concept of ownership is also very important. Up to now, in all possibility, the major events in a young person's life will have been driven by someone else, such as the family holiday which is usually organized by parents. Now, possibly for the first time, the young person has participated in an event which they have helped to plan, without parental involvement and, most importantly, one with which they have, hopefully, been involved at every stage in the process from concept to completion.

I have termed the condition post-residential syndrome (rather than post-adventure syndrome or something similar) because the concept of some form of residential setting is a major key to the process of Outdoor Education. The residential, whether this be nights spent under canvas or time in a mountain centre or hostel, allows the young people to function as a team across all aspects of their personal and social development. The notion of caring for each other, and sharing chores such as cooking and washing up, is crucial for each individual taking responsibility

197

for their own actions with all members having an equally important role to play in the process. The residential setting also allows opportunities for the reflective processes of review and evaluation to take place, whether prompted by a leader or, more informally, by the group chatting over their day's experiences. Through these processes, of shared experiences, the event becomes more meaningful and does not become merely a short term 'fairground ride' of instant excitement. Parallels could, of course, be drawn to the camaraderie of athletes living together in the Olympic Village or to the Dunkirk spirit of people living under the threat of the blitz. Although, as we saw earlier, post-traumatic stress affects many who served in combat, many veterans and civilian survivors of the World Wars feel, in retrospect, that their wartime experiences were the highpoint of their lives.

The recognition by outdoor educationalists that post-residential syndrome exists is an important ingredient in the young persons' overall enjoyment of the experience. All too often, as discussed in an excellent chapter entitled 'Thoughts on party leadership' in *Mountaincraft and Leadership* by Ken Ogilvie (1984), the concept of group leadership is based on factors to be considered 'before' and 'during' the venture; however, as was stressed in Chapter 4, the 'after' is equally as important. A vital part of the planning for the final venture should, therefore, be the organization of events to follow the expedition so that the emotions are let down gradually in the same way as an athlete 'warms down' after a strenuous event. Olympic athletes do not do a lap of honour simply to wave to the crowds; they are giving their muscles a chance to gradually relax and their bodies time to compose themselves after being high on adrenaline for the big event. We should, therefore, plan when the group will meet together a couple of weeks after returning from the venture to reflect on the experience and produce some form of report; when duplicate photos will be ordered and collected; when a presentation of their report will be made, and to whom. Perhaps organize a reunion get-together or meal, and why not invite all those involved in the planning, sponsorship and support functions of the venture (even if they were not present during the event itself) who would also like to share in the experience. Will there be another similar venture next year for another group of young people from the same locality? Would these new youngsters like to hear about the group's experiences or see the slides – especially if you were lucky enough for the venture to take place in Europe or further abroad.

The understanding of post-residential syndrome and the provision of after-care facilities for young people returning from an adventurous experience (whether or not the venture was a success, although imperative if it was not) should become an integral part of the provision of Outdoor Education. As was seen in Chapter 4, successful Outdoor Education is an ongoing process with several significant stages and the debrief, evaluation and reviewing of the experience undertaken during the reflective stage is one of, if not the, most important elements. Although all ventures should, ideally, involve ongoing reflection and the processing of experiences, there should, at the end, be a complete recording of events. As well as satisfying the innate human characteristic of storytelling, March and Wattchow suggest that the reporting/reflective/processing phase allows participants to report on their adventure to others, to provide information to assist further ventures and to seek enjoyment through entertaining peers with tales of their exploits. More importantly, they feel that the reportage 'provides a sense of closure to the expedition, eases the stress of re-entry into society, enhances personal growth, and is often the birth place for future ventures' (March and Wattchow, 1991, p. 4).

The review of the experience among their peers is, therefore, sufficient for the majority of participants to 'talk through' the events and adventures in which they have taken part and to arrest the onset of post-residential syndrome. This has the important bonus of providing a mutual support system so that the experience can have a positive and life-enhancing effect on everyone's personal growth. Certainly any unplanned aspect of the venture, such as groups getting lost and righting themselves or equipment not performing as expected, should be reviewed to see what lessons can be learnt from the events, and it is crucial that any form of personality clash or breakdown in group dynamics is talked through on a calm and rational level.

The shared experience and memories will remain, but the highly charged feelings will gradually fade away over the course of time. Hopefully participants will get involved in ventures, projects and journeys of their own, or return to help with training new youngsters taking part in future ventures. Most importantly, their experience and enthusiasm should not be lost. The adventurous experience should be a means to an end rather than an end in itself.

A doorway rather than a barrier

Young people should not feel that their involvement in the outdoors has ceased, or has in any way been restricted, by the ending of one particular experience. As part of the training process, they should have gained the enlightenment to realize that they themselves have the tools – in terms of motivation and organizational ability – to plan and execute ventures of their own. To this end, it is important that all structured programmes of Outdoor Education are progressive in nature, with the participants' initial excursions into the outdoors taking place within easy reach of their home base. All urban conurbations have areas of open countryside surrounding them which provide ample opportunities for entry-level activities such as orienteering, mountainbiking, canoeing, rowing or sailing on canal, river or lake and, even, rock-climbing now that most big towns have excellent purpose-built artificial climbing walls. The young people must learn that, within a bus journey, or cycle ride, are myriad opportunities for them to undertake exciting and adventurous activities and that they are not dependent upon a planned venture for continuing their involvement in the outdoors.

It cannot be educationally viable for a major overseas expedition to pluck youngsters from inner-city areas, and take them on a fantastically exciting residential experience to a remote corner of the world, only to – some weeks or months later – deposit them back into their old surroundings. They will have seen that an adventurous world exists, but will not have been provided with access to it. In such cases, young people would soon develop the symptoms of stress associated with post-residential syndrome and would, in all probability, be dissatisfied with their old lifestyle and surroundings. This need not be the case, inner cities have much to offer. The majority of climbing and mountaineering clubs are based in towns and cities, making regular planned visits to wild country areas, and most clubs welcome young and enthusiastic members. Allow young people the ability to follow the advice of Professor Cooper and, if all else fails, and post-experience blues are really getting you down, cheer yourself up by planning your next sunny break. Many of us involved in the outdoors would agree that the best time to plan your next expedition is while away on the current one!

As educationalists we have a duty to ensure that, whatever the exact activity around which the adventurous experienced is based, it is part of a continuum of involvement. The best compliment we could ever be paid, in illustrating the success of our nurturing of the young into challenging outdoor activities and for providing total quality across the whole experience, would be if our young people, in the fullness of time as parents, were able to introduce their own children to the excitement of the outdoors.

A total package of care

We have a responsibility, therefore, to accept that post-residential syndrome may possibly occur and, subsequently, play an important role in ensuring that its effects are minimized. We should plan for the participants being slightly depressed on their re-entry to normal life, after the adventurous experience, and treat their reactions sympathetically. We, as leaders, should take on the function of being a conduit for the young people's future involvement in a possible lifetime of enjoyment and fulfilment in the outdoors and help them into this by having access to reference material such as clubs and societies to which they could become affiliated. This is part and parcel of our role. The duty of care which we exercise so vigorously should not just apply to the young people's physical safety during the expedition, but extend to their emotional well-being after the event. Make the effort, therefore, to set aside time during the preparation stages of the venture to plan a 'warm down' phase after the event so that you all, leaders and participants alike, can have an opportunity to re-live your experiences and reflect on the achievement of a task well done.

However, a word of warning. Heed the advice given in Chapter 4, do not try and do all this on your own. Enlist the help of another leader who will have the specific responsibility of arranging the reunion and any other events. You will have invested heavily, emotionally, in the adventure, so do not spread yourself too thinly. Otherwise, the only victim of post-residential syndrome could well be you!

Conclusion

The truth of the matter is that, thankfully, the overwhelming majority of Outdoor Education is undertaken sensitively and professionally (with a small 'p') by adults and agencies with a genuine concern for the continuing development of young people. Although many leaders may never have intentionally planned it that way, the operation of many of the varied forms of outdoor experience available to young people naturally provides a support structure for the participants long after the activity itself has been and gone. Well-conducted Outdoor Education is seen as a continuous process and mutual support is standard practice; it is rare for young people to be left in a vacuum.

There is always common ground between the participants and leaders as, no matter what role the individual played in the planning of the venture or in the management of the experience, they were all in it together. Perhaps that is one of the strengths of the voluntary nature of much outdoor work, as mentioned in the opening chapters. When both sides – the leaders and the led – are there because they have chosen to be there, out of their own free will, a strong bond of commonality is formed. Standing around a flickering stove in a wet and windy campsite, waiting for a brew, both sides know, deep down, that they could always choose not to be there! But they do not. In most cases previous experiences and adventures are recounted with fondness and thoughts turn to the next venture; always onwards and upwards. The outdoors provides an arena for emotional, mental and spiritual, as well as physical space and this extends further and deeper into our psyche than just for the duration of an individual expedition or trip.

Outdoor Education is uplifting, fun and exciting, as well as being challenging, and it allows us an opportunity to escape from the confines of everyday life and, for that reason alone, to my mind, it is worth it. In a letter to all those who had assisted with the consultation process for the production of *In Search of Adventure*, Lord Hunt stated that, from his own experience, he was convinced that

> we could and should do more to develop the potential human qualities of our youth than is the case at present. They are, in an important sense, our most valuable asset, and many of them deserve a better chance to enjoy leisure time in beneficial ways. (Hunt, 1989a)

We have, as outdoor educationalists, the tools at our disposal to develop this valuable asset through a medium which is educationally, socially and, of increasing consequence, financially viable. Surely future generations deserve the chance to savour learning in a natural environment, undertaking challenging activities through their own endeavours? Even if it is only the fact that this provides an opportunity to do something of individual value, away from the influences of everyday life. As Robert Frost (1874–1963) said in the last verse of his poem 'The Road Not Taken':

I shall be telling this with a sigh
Somewhere ages and ages hence:
Two roads diverged in a wood, and I –
I took the one less travelled by,
And that has made all the difference.
(from *The Poetry of Robert Frost*,
ed. Edward Connery Latham, published by Jonathan Cape)

To provide young people, through Outdoor Education, with opportunities to take responsibility for their own actions and well-being is a significant stimulus and one which may have consequences lasting for the rest of their lives.

Useful addresses

British Mountaineering Council
177–179 Burton Road
West Didsbury
Manchester, M20 2BB

Council for Outdoor Education, Training and Recreation
Bowles Outdoor Education Centre
Erridge Green
Tunbridge Wells
Kent TN3 9LW

The Duke of Edinburgh's Award
Gulliver House
Madeira Walk
Windsor
Berkshire, SL4 1EU

Foundation for Outdoor Adventure
Muncaster Country Guest House
Muncaster
Ravenglass
Cumbria, CA18 1RD

National Association for Outdoor Education
12 St Andrews Churchyard
Penrith
Cumbria, CA 11 7YE

Outdoor Education

Outward Bound Trust
Watermillock
Nr. Penrith
Cumbria, CA11 0JL

UK Mountain Training Board
Capel Curig
Gwynedd, LL24 0ET

Young Explorers Trust
c/o Royal Geographical Society
1 Kensington Gore
London, SW7 2AR

Bibliography

Adair, J. (1986) *Effective Teambuilding*, Aldershot: Gower.

Adair, J. (1988) *Developing Leaders*, Guildford: Talbot Adair Press.

Adair, J. (1988a) *Effective Leadership*, rev. edn, London: Pan Books.

Adams, J. (1995) *Risk*, London: University College London Press.

American Psychiatric Association (1980) *Diagnostic and Statistical Manual of Mental Disorders*, 3rd edn, Washington DC.

Austin, C. (1993) 'Knocking heads together', *Professional Manager*, 2(3).

Bakshian, A. Jr (1996) *Your Guide to Successful Speaking*, Washington DC: Georgetown Publishing.

Ball, S. (1990) *Politics and Policy Making in Education: Explorations in Policy Sociology*, London: Routledge.

Barton, R. (1994) 'Outward but not bounders', *Times Educational Supplement*, 4 February.

Beardsley, T. (1994) 'Up with the birds', *Times Educational Supplement*, 4 February.

Beaumont, P. and Douglas, E. (1995) 'Mother of all mountains, father of all obsessions', *Observer*, 20 August.

Belbin, M. (1983) *Management Teams: Why They Succeed or Fail*, Oxford: Butterworth Heinemann.

Bond, M. (1997) 'One man, three camels, 1,000 miles too far', *The Times*, 8 January.

Bonington, C. (1994) 'The heights of teamwork', *Personnel Management*, October.

Boud, D., Cohen, R. and Walker, D. (1993) *Using Experience for Learning*, SRHE, Open University Press.

Bradford Council Directorate of Education (BCDE) (1994) *Safety Document for Outdoor Activities*. Bradford: Directorate of Education.

Coles, M. (1997) 'Am I a good manager?', *Sunday Times*, 26 January.

207

Crisp, Q. (1996) 'The only emotion to be sure of is fear', *Guardian*, 6 December.

de Bono, E. (1977) *Lateral Thinking*, London: Pelican.

Dearlove, D. (1995) 'Do personality tests work?', *The Times*, 27 July.

Department for Education and Employment (DfEE) (1995) *Safety in Outdoor Education*, London: HMSO.

Department of Education and Science (1975) 'Outdoor education: The report of the Dartington Hall Conference' (N496), London: Mimeo.

Doherty, N. and Horsted, J. (1995) 'Helping survivors stay on board', *People Management*, 12 January.

Doidge, J., Bone, D. and Hardwick, R. (1996) *Quality Teams: Leader Guide and Workbook*, Sheffield: UK Universities and Colleges Staff Development Agency.

Driscoll, M. (1997) 'Against all odds', *Sunday Times*, 12 January.

Duke of Edinburgh's Award (1981) *Expedition Guide for Temperate Climates*, London.

Duke of Edinburgh's Award (1996) 'Something else', in *Assessor's Log Book*, pp. 2. 12 – 2. 18.

Ford, R. (1995) 'Offenders to take adventure courses', *The Times*, 12 July.

Frost, R. (1971) *The Poetry of Robert Frost*. London: Jonathan Cape.

Frost, W. (1997) 'A passion for high adventure', *The Times*, 8 January.

Gane, D. (1995) 'Teachers sacked after losing child on day trip', *The Times*, 26 September.

Goldstein, R. (1994) 'The back to work blues', *Mail on Sunday*, 4 September.

Golzen, G. (1993) 'Team up for business success', *Sunday Times*, 21 February.

Gruner, P. (1992) 'You need a rest to get over a holiday', *Evening Standard*, 10 July.

Hansard (1993) 'Unqualified teachers', *Written Answers* cols 231–2, 20 July.

Hastings, C., Bixby, P. and Chaudry-Lawton, R. (1994) *Superteams: Building Organizational Success through High-Performing Teams*, London: HarperCollins.

Haughton, E. (1993) 'Sense of involvement', *Personnel Today*, 29 June.

Hawkes, N. (1995) 'Personality test could help keep soccer players on the ball', *The Times*, 26 June.

Health and Safety Commission (HSC) (1995) *Proposals for Regulations and Guidance to Implement the Safety Provisions of the Activity Centres (Young Persons' Safety) Act 1995*, London: HSC.

Health and Safety Executive (HSE) (1996) *Guidance to the Licensing Authority on the Adventure Activities Licensing Regulations 1996 (Guidance on Regulations)*, London: HMSO.

Holt, J. (1969) *How Children Fail*, London: Penguin.

Hopkins, D. and Putnam, R. (1993) *Personal Growth through Adventure*, London: David Fulton.

Hore, M. (1994) *Times Educational Supplement*, 4 February.

Hoyle, E. and John, P. D. (1995) *Professional Knowledge and Professional Practice*, London: Cassell.

HRH The Duke of Edinburgh (1996) Speech given at The Duke of Edinburgh's Award General Council Conference, Birmingham, 14 November.

Hulse, S. (1995) 'Bean stalkers fail on the fells', *Guardian*, 4 April.

Hunt, Lord J. (ed.) (1989) *In Search of Adventure*, Guildford: Talbot Adair Press.

Hunt, Lord J. (1989a) Personal letter, September.

Hutchings, I. (1993) 'Appraisal procedure: a recipe for mediocrity?', *New Academic*, 2(3).

Iwerrah, A. (1996) Speech given at The Duke of Edinburgh's Award General Council Conference, Birmingham, 14 November.

Johnstone, H. (1995) 'Everest conqueror shares triumph with her children', *The Times*, 15 May.

Keay, W. (1989) *Land Navigation: Routefinding with Map and Compass*, London: The Duke of Edinburgh's Award.

Keay, W. (1996) *Expedition Guide*, London: The Duke of Edinburgh's Award.

Keighley, P. W. (1988) 'The future place of Outdoor Education in the context of the National Curriculum', *Journal of Adventure Education and Outdoor Leadership*, 5(2).

Knight, K. (1994) 'School head tells of survivors' trauma', *The Times*, 9 December.

Knight, K. (1995) 'Untrained climbing instructor jailed', *The Times*, 8 February.

Kolb, D. (1984) *Experiential Learning*, Englewood Cliffs, New Jersey: Prentice Hall.

Landale, J. (1995) 'Soldiers executed in the Great War may be pardoned', *The Times*, 16 September.

Lee, A. (1996) 'Refs face liability after injury ruling', *The Times*, 18 December.

Lee, K. A., Vaillant, G. E., Torrey, W. C. and Elder, G. H. (1995) 'A 50-year prospective study of the psychological sequelae of World War II combat', *American Journal of Psychiatry*, 152(4), p. 516.

Lennon, P. (1993) 'The perils of snow business', *Guardian*, 30 August.

Lewis, D. (1994) 'Why do we risk it?', *Focus Magazine*, Summer.

Lowenstein, L. (1991) 'Teaching stress leading to burnout', *Education Today*, 41(2).

Loynes, C. (1996) 'Editorial', *Adventure Education and Outdoor Leadership*, 13(1).

March, W. and Wattchow, B. (1991) 'The importance of the expedition in adventure education', *Journal of Adventure Education*, 8(2).

Maslow, A. H. (1968) *Toward a Psychology of Being*, 2nd edn, New York: van Nostrand.

Maxwell Magnus, S. (1995) 'Taking on the agony', *Guardian*, 1 July.

McWhirter, J. (1996) *New Reporter*, 13(20), University of Southampton.

Mihill, C. (1995) 'Non-academic skills "key to success"', *Guardian*, 9 June.

Mihill, C. (1996) 'Sports myth scotched', *Guardian*, 12 December.

Mortlock, C. (1984) *The Adventure Alternative*, Milnthorpe, Cumbria: Cicerone Press.

Mungham, G. and Pearson, G. (1976) *Working Class Youth Culture*, London: Routledge and Kegan Paul.

National Association for Outdoor Education (1996) *NAOE Newsletter* (21), Autumn.

National Association for Outdoor Education (NAOE) (1981) *The Curriculum*, Penrith: Cumbria: NAOE.

O'Brien, T. (1995) *Observer*, 11 June.

O'Connor, B. (1995) *The Times*, 15 May.

O'Leary, J. (1997) 'After-school activities help pupils to improve grades', *The Times*, 15 January.

Office of Population Censuses and Surveys (OPCS) (1992) *OPCS Monitor*, DH4 93/3, London: Government Statistical Service.

Ogilvie, K. (1984) 'Thoughts on party leadership', *Mountaincraft and Leadership*, Edinburgh: Mountainwalking Leader Training Board.

Ogilvie, K. (1996) *Leading and Managing Groups in the Outdoors*, Edinburgh: National Association for Outdoor Education.

Outdoor Education – Safety and Good Practice (1988) Association of Heads of Outdoor Education Centres, National Association of Field Studies Officers, National Association for Outdoor Education, Outdoor Education Advisers Panel, and the Scottish Panel for

Advisers in Outdoor Education, published by The Duke of Edinburgh's Award, London.

Outdoor Education and the National Curriculum (1990) Association of Heads of Outdoor Education Centres, National Association for Outdoor Education, Outdoor Education Advisers Panel, and the Scottish Panel for Advisers in Outdoor Education, April.

Owens, R. (1996) 'It's all go on active service', *Guardian*, 28 August.

Paffard, M. (1973) *Inglorious Wordsworths*, London: Hodder and Stoughton.

Peters, R. S. (1966) *Ethics and Education*, London: Allen and Unwin.

Pilkington, E. and Moss, S. (1994) 'Spoil sport', *Guardian*, 1 March.

Radford, T. (1994) 'Anti-freeze diet', *Guardian*, 15 March.

Royal County of Berkshire (RCB) (1989) *Report of the Altwood School Inquiry Panel*, January. Reading: RCB County Council.

Royal Society Study Group (1983) *Risk Assessment*, report of The Royal Society, London, January.

Royal Society Study Group (1992) *Risk: Analysis, Perception and Management*, report of The Royal Society, London.

Rutter, M. and Smith, D. J. (1996) *Psychosocial Disorders in Young People*, Chichester: John Wiley.

Schön, D. (1983) *The Reflective Practitioner: How Professionals Think in Action*, Aldershot: Arena.

Smart, J. and Watson, G. (1995) *Educational Visits*, Leamington Spa: Campion Communications.

Stroud, M. (1994) *Shadows on the Wasteland*, London: Penguin.

Stuttaford, T. (1997) 'Danger brings out the best and the worst', *The Times*, 8 January.

Surrey County Council (SCC) (1991) *Outdoor Education Policy*. Surrey County Council.

The Head's Legal Guide (1993) Kingston upon Thames: Croner.

The Sheffield Study (1995) London: The Sports' Council.

Turner, M. T. (1994) *Times Educational Supplement*, 4 February.

UK Mountain Training Board (UKMTB) (1995) *National Guidelines: Advice on Safety, Good Practice and the Use of Mountain Training Awards*, Capel Curig, North Wales: UKMTB.

Wessely, S. (1995) 'From shell shock to combat fatigue', *The Times*, 4 May.

Whapham, J. (1995) *Guardian*, 1 July.

White, J. (1997) 'Calls of the wild', *Guardian*, 8 January.

Wolf, J. (1994) 'Riding for a fall', *Times Educational Supplement*, 4 February.

211

Index

212